STRESS
AND
RELAXATION

STRESS
AND
RELAXATION

LESLIE KENTON

Books
UK
Ltd.

First published 1986
by Century Hutchinson Ltd
Brookmount House, 62-65 Chandos Place
London WC2N 4NW

Reprinted 1989

Century Hutchinson Australia (Pty) Ltd
89–91 Albion Street, Surry Hills, NSW 2010

Century Hutchinson New Zealand Ltd
PO Box 40-086, Glenfield, Auckland 10, New Zealand

Century Hutchinson South Africa (Pty) Ltd
PO Box 337, Bergvlei, 2012 South Africa

ISBN 0-7126-9533-8

Edited, designed and produced by The Paul Press Ltd,
22 Bruton Street, London W1X 7DA

Project Editor Linda Sonntag
Art Editor David Ayres
Illustrations Chris Chapman, Jacek Depczyk
Picture Research Liz Eddison
Art Director Stephen McCurdy
Editorial Director Jeremy Harwood
Publishing Director Nigel Perryman

Typeset by Wordsmiths, Street, Somerset
Origination by London Offset Colour Ltd
Printed in Singapore
by Toppan Printing Company

CONTENTS

INTRODUCTION

Stress and relaxation are two sides of the same coin. If stress gets out of hand it can wear you down, ruin your looks and destroy your inner peace, but there are ways of turning it into a positive force in your life. The key to stress management is conscious relaxation.

Just as stretching your body to its physical limits through exercise is a way of widening awareness of what is possible for you, so practising conscious relaxation is a key to your depths. It will uncover physical and mental potential you didn't know you possessed. Like both exercise and optimum nutrition, it will increase the energy available to you enormously.

Learning a few techniques for letting go and practising them daily can do something else even more important: it can help you get in touch with the very centre of your being, which is probably more important to the discovery of your own individual beauty than any other single thing. Here at the centre is where the discovery of your self begins. This discovery and the expression of this self in how you move and talk, think and feel, work and relate to others, is what real beauty is all about.

Relaxation practised daily can also unlock new ways of responding to what happens at home, at work, and in relationships with the rest of the world. It can help you discover new, more creative ways of looking at things and free you from mechanical patterns of thinking and living which – although you may be unaware of them – destroy your feeling of aliveness. Finally, it can bring you a delightful sense of serenity.

First, we'll take a look at how stress and relaxation relate to each other and at how to make stress work for, rather than against you. Then we'll explore the possibilities of relaxing the mind and examine the reasons why sleep is so important to health and beauty. Next we'll turn our attention to body relaxation. We'll see how the way you breathe affects the way you feel. We'll take a good look at the benefits of yoga with a sequence that's designed to gently stretch each part of your body. We'll go through a revitalizing massage routine that's as absorbing to give as it is to receive, and venture into the less-known worlds of shiatsu and reflexology. And, in addition there's some helpful advice on nutrition and diet.

UNDERSTANDING STRESS

It is now common knowledge that uncontrolled stress can trigger a great many diseases and disorders – insomnia, gastric ulcers, high blood pressure, asthma, and migraine, to mention just a few. But for a long time these ailments were treated like something over which we had no control. It was assumed that one could only treat their symptoms with drugs, treat the stress that triggered them off with more drugs, and hope for the best. Now, thanks to research into altered states of consciousness and work done with biofeedback, studies have shown that every human being can exercise a high level of conscious control over his nervous system. They have shown that we do indeed have the ability to release excessive nervous tension, provided we train ourselves to do it. They have also shown that when this excessive nervous tension is released, the physical and psychological effects of stress are significantly reduced. The key to this control is relaxation. It can eliminate digestive disorders, lower cholestrol levels in the blood, improve sleep, make reducing easier and even speed up healing in your body.

HOW THE NERVOUS SYSTEM WORKS

Most of the automatic, or involuntary, functions of your body are governed by a part of the nervous system known as the autonomic nervous system. It looks after the changes in the rate at which your heart beats. It regulates your blood pressure by altering the size of veins and arteries. It stimulates the flow of digestive juices and brings on muscular contractions in the digestive system to deal with the foods you take in. It makes you sweat when you're hot and is responsible for the physical changes in your body that come with sexual arousal. This autonomic system has two opposing branches: the sympathetic and the parasympathetic.

The sympathetic branch is composed of a group of nerve fibres radiating from the spinal cord and is linked with the catecholamines or adrenalin class of hormones. It is concerned with energy expenditure – particularly the energy involved with stress. It spurs the heart to beat faster, makes you breathe hard, encourages you to sweat, and raises your blood pressure. It also inhibits the secretion of gastric juices and digestion and sends blood to the muscles to get you ready for action.

The other branch of the autonomic nervous

system - the parasympathetic - is made up mostly of nerve fibres from the vagus nerve, or tenth cranial. Its activity is linked with the acetylcholine class of hormones, and this system is concerned with rest rather than action. In fact, the 'workings of the parasympathetic branch are more or less in opposition to those of the sympathetic branch. The parasympathetic branch slows your heartbeat, reduces the flow of air to your lungs, stimulates the digestive system, and helps relax your muscles.

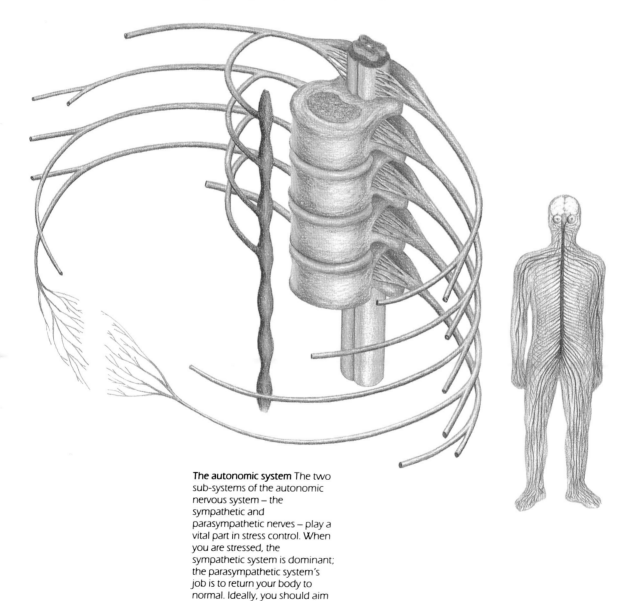

The autonomic system The two sub-systems of the autonomic nervous system – the sympathetic and parasympathetic nerves – play a vital part in stress control. When you are stressed, the sympathetic system is dominant; the parasympathetic system's job is to return your body to normal. Ideally, you should aim at a balance between the two.

GETTING THE BALANCE RIGHT

When you are in a state of stress, the sympathetic nervous system has precedence over the parasympathetic. When you are relaxed, the parasympathetic branch is dominant. A good balance between the two is the key to enormous energy and continuing health. Balance makes it possible for you

Stress versus relaxation
Stress and relaxation are complementary opposite states, and both are necessary for a balanced life lived to the full. Stress, whether caused by pressure at work or emotional problems, can actually be used to advantage, if you practise conscious methods of relaxation as an antidote. Think of it as charging your batteries, then letting go and freewheeling.

to go out into the world to do, to make, to create, to fight, and to express yourself as well as to retire into yourself for regeneration, rest, recuperation, enjoyment, and the space to discover new ideas and plant the seeds of future actions. Unfortunately few people get the balance right.

Instead, there is the dynamic liberated woman who is always seeking greater challenges and heights of personal achievement and who seems to have endless energy – until she discovers in a few years that she is suffering from high blood pressure and is told either to ease up or to go into long-term drug therapy for hypertension. At the other extreme is the beautifully feminine, quiet, sensitive lady who luxuriates in physical comforts, dreams beautiful dreams, and impresses everyone by her serenity but who never seems to be able to put any of her ideas into effective action.

The first is a sympathetic-dominated person and the second is parasympathetic-dominated. To make the most of your potential in action in the world and still remain well enough and receptive enough to enjoy the fruits of your labours, you want to be neither. You need to be balanced. That's where learning the art of conscious relaxation comes in.

For, like the sympathetic and the parasympathetic branches of the autonomic nervous system which oppose each other, there is nothing vague or unclear about what constitutes a state of stress and its opposite, a state of psychophysical relaxation. These states are like two sides of the same coin. The biochemical and psychological changes that accompany each can be accurately measured in a laboratory.

STRESS VERSUS RELAXATION

Under stress your body consumes more oxygen, its metabolic rate increases, your arteries contract, the concentration of lactates in your blood goes up, and your heart beats faster. During stress, cortisone levels in the body are increased. Over a long period of time this tends to block out the immune response; this is one of the main reasons why you become less resistant to disease when you go into a state of psychophysical relaxation: cardiac rate decreases, lactate levels fall, there is a decrease in oxygen consumption, and your body returns to a regenerative state. Here are a few of the measurable differences between the two states:

	IN STRESS The action of the sympathetic branch of the autonomic nervous system is dominant	IN PSYCHOPHYSICAL RELAXATION The action of the autonomic nervous system is dominant
heartbeat rate	raised	lowered
blood flow to muscles	increased	decreased
blood flow to organs	increased	decreased
demand for oxygen	increased	decreased
cortisone output	increased	decreased
blood pressure	increased	decreased
muscle tension	increased	decreased
	THE RESULT Readiness for action	THE RESULT Proper functioning of body's organs and systems

The secret of getting the right balance between stress and relaxation, between the sympathetic and the parasympathetic branches is twofold. First you need to take a look at the stress in your life and discover new ways of using it positively. Second, you need to learn a technique for conscious relaxation and practise it daily until it becomes second nature. Not only will this help your body stay in balance and increase your level of overall vitality, it will also give you a profound sense of control over yourself and your life that is hard to come by any other way. Let's look at stress first.

MAKE FRIENDS WITH STRESS

Long-term stress can destroy your good looks, your vitality and eventually your health. But contrary to popular belief, that doesn't mean there is anything intrinsically dangerous in stress. On the contrary, stress is the spice of life – the challenge just waiting to be met, the excitement of something new and unknown, the wonderful, exhilarating feeling when adrenalin flows through your body and makes you feel ready for anything. It only means that if you do not know how to move from the active, stressed state of mind and body into the passive state of psychophysical relaxation at will, then you, like most people (for few have this skill naturally), are likely to find yourself stuck in the stressed state for long periods. And if it happens often enough and lasts long enough, you can become physically or mentally ill.

THE FIGHT OR FLIGHT MECHANISM

Human beings are natural seekers of challenge. In primitive times the challenge was one of survival, and this gave a certain rhythm to the working of the body. When in danger from some external cause – say, a wild animal – the body reacted instantaneously, providing the energy resources to fight or flee. The physiological changes brought about in the body by stressors are described as the 'fight or flight mechanism'. Adrenal secretions flash into the blood and bring strength in the form of fat and sugar energy to the brain and muscles. The pulse races, blood pressure increases, and breathing speeds up. Within seconds the body's full energy potential is realized, so one can deal effectively with the threat – either by fighting and destroying it or by running away to safety. Both actions use up all the chemical by-products of the stress reaction – the sugar, the adrenalin, and the increased muscle strength that accompanies them.

When the danger passes, the body relaxes. The production of adrenalin slows to a trickle and heartbeat and breathing decrease. The body returns to its vegetative rhythm, restoring normality to physiological processes and bringing a sense of mental and physical well-being.

We are biologically the same creatures as those who dealt with wild animals. Our bodies still react to danger in the same way, but now our sense of danger comes from different threats. They can be the pressures of deadlines for work, the fear that someone is trying to take your job from you, or worry about losing the closeness of the man you

Fight or flight When danger threatens, all the senses are alerted.

Your senses – primarily the eyes and ears – warn you of danger by passing impulses down the sensory nerves to the brain.

In response to the warnings it has received, the brain sends out a set of nerve impulses. These travel down the spinal cord through the motor nerves to the muscles of the body.

When the signals reach the nerve endings in the muscles, a chemical transmittor is released. This stimulates the muscles' contraction. At the same time, the sympathetic nerves divert fuel and oxygen to the tissues involved.

At the same time that eyes and ears are warning the brain of potential danger, sensors in the muscles and joints alert it to the position and preparedness of the body.

Simultaneously, the autonomic nerves come into play. They stimulate the heartbeat, dilate the bronchi, so allowing more air to reach the lungs, and dilate the pupils of the eyes, inhibit disgestion, relax the bladder and dilate the blood vessels of the muscles, so increasing their blood supply.

love if you do what you really want to do instead of what he wants. All these, and many other things too cause a women to move into the danger rhythm state without suffering physical or mental damage.

The trouble is that modern life, with its noise, quick pace, social pressures, environmental poisons, and our orientation to sedentary mental work, presents many of us with almost constant threat situations. This is particularly true in the business world where a woman, instead of moving rhythmically out of the danger state into the vegetative one, remains for long periods (in some cases, all her waking hours) in the danger state with all the internal physical conditions that accompany it: her blood pressure rarely goes down to normal, her pulse remains rapid, and her muscles and brain are activated by the production of adrenalin but she has no physical outlets for this increased energy. Sooner or later, unless she is moved out of the threatening situation, she, the predator who at one time preyed on the wild beast, begins to prey internally on herself.

STRESS MANAGEMENT

One of the most serious by-products of this kind of stress is the tension it produces. When you are under prolonged stress, you unconsciously tense different parts of your body. This affects not only the muscles, but also the organs themselves – gall bladder, liver, kidneys, even the area of the heart and lungs. In time this kind of tension restricts circulation to the organs and also prevents proper nutrient assimilation by the cells, encouraging their breakdown and early ageing. This, and the fact that the increased cortisone levels that accompany stress tend to knock out the body's immune response, is why stress is at the very least a contributory factor to many contemporary ailments including ulcers, high blood pressure, arthritis constricted blood vessels, and heart disease. Recently it has also been linked with cancer.

Because everyone's stress level is different, and because stress taken to extremes depletes your body not only of its resistance but eventually of its life energy, stress is also a major factor in ageing. In fact, one of the main theories of ageing states that the body is able to withstand only so much stress and no more and the faster this is used up, the faster it ages.

MAKING STRESS WORK FOR YOU

But the idea that all stress is bad is patent nonsense. As human beings we would be little more than vegetables without some stress in our lives. Also, and more important, the more committed we are to the lives we are leading and the more right they are for us, the less likely we are to suffer the ravages of stress.

The women most susceptible to stress damage include those inclined to psychosomatic illness resulting from the constant conflict between what they are by nature and what, as a result of social and cultural pressures, they try to appear. This seems to me a particular problem of the twentieth century, for the current cultural and psychological stereotypes of feminity and womanliness can be heavy burdens to bear. They often have little to do with the true character of a particular woman – little to do with the self – although conditioning and the will to please have often made many women accept them. But it works the other way too: many of the more dynamic, aggressive women who have striven to shed these stereotypes have their own burdens to carry in the image of the hard-driving, liberated female always eager for new challenges and always moving forward. For like a piece of elastic constantly stretched, they can eventually snap or only partly return to normal. So even those who by their nature seek out challenges eventually wear out. Nobody can live under constant strain. And any image one is forced to uphold causes unnecessary strain and destroy's one's ability to enjoy and find meaning in one's life.

So in personal terms, for the sake of mental and physical health and beauty it is important that every woman develops an awareness of her own personal relationship to stress and comes to terms with it. This is all part of what is known as 'stress management'. There are many different methods of going about it. If you are familiar with them you can choose which ones work best for you and you will be able to live with stress and actually enjoy it.

REALIZE THAT YOU ARE IN CONTROL

You have all the inner resources necessary to deal with any situation that may arise. But do you know it? Stressors are neutral, neither good nor bad. They simply are, and they call for some kind of action. Your response to them and the stress they trigger in you is entirely dependent on you. It is inside you, not the result of some outside force. And it is in your power to decide clearly whether you are going to face the challenge and see it through, so that stress becomes a stimulus to your well-being, or whether you are going to allow yourself to shrink from it and let it turn to distress. Marcus Aurelius put this very well when he said, 'If you are distressed by anything external, the pain is not due to the thing itself but to your estimate of it.' This you have the power to revoke at any time. Taking stock of your own power and realizing that you alone have the ability to control whether your stress responses will be positive or negative can lead you to look at stress in a positive way, so that instead of succumbing to misery and despair in which you experience biochemical reactions that are harmful to your body, you can, each time you face a stressor, be strengthened by it and find it an exciting challenge.

GET TO KNOW THE PHYSICAL ANTIDOTES TO STRESS

And use them when you need to. Besides a nutritionally adequate diet that includes plenty of fibre from whole grains and raw fruit and vegetables, you can take supplements of vitamin C, the B complex, lecithin, calcium and vitamin E.

A classic anti-stress supplement formula available from health food stores is 500 milligrams of vitamin C, coupled with 100 milligrams of pantothenic acid, 20 milligrams each of B6 and B2 and the rest of the B-complex range in the same tablet or taken in the form of brewer's yeast. Vitamin C and pantothenic acid help protect the adrenal glands from damage. Liver is an excellent food to eat when you are under particular stress, both because of its B-complex content and because it is rich in vitamin A, another substance known to strengthen the body's resistance to illness and allergic reactions that can be stress induced. As will be seen in the diet section, the need for vitamin C and the B-complex range increases when you are in stressful situations of any kind, whether caused by emotional strain, excessive exertion, fatigue, internal pollution by poisons, drugs or alcohol, illness or even falling in love.

Vitamins C and E are also useful in detoxifying your body and protecting it from the potential harm of stress-generating chemicals. And it is important that you don't let yourself get overweight, which reduces your capacity for dealing with stress, that you take regular exercise, which helps burn up the by-products of stress in the body so that they are rendered harmless, and that you take a holiday 'away from it all' often enough.

USING STRESS IN YOUR RELATIONSHIP

Find out how many different principles and ways of managing stress you can successfully incorporate into your life. Then do it. Stress in a relationship can be a way of improving not only the quality of the relationship but also the value that one places on it. This demands facing discontent clearly and squarely and expressing it in a way that doesn't try to make someone else responsible for it. For instance, there are two ways of complaining when your mate squeezes the toothpaste in the middle. One is, 'My God you did it again. What's wrong with you?' and the other, 'You know I have a problem. I am really bothered by people squeezing the toothpaste in the middle. I can't seem to get over it. I'd be grateful if you didn't do it. It would help me a lot.'

Another thing it demands is looking at every relationship as it really is, rather than as you would like it to be; also it means being aware of your own needs and expressing them clearly and openly instead of being quietly resentful that they are not met automatically by others.

It will help protect you from stress if you learn to deal with one thing at a time – living in the immediate present which, after all, is the only time you can really know, rather than worrying about the future too much. The past is completely dead. Only now exists. Knowing this can immediately transform a lot of distress into simple, exhilarating stress.

LEARNING TO TURN OFF

There are scores of effective techniques for quieting the mind and recreating the calm serenity that puts you more and more in touch with your own creative centre. They include autogenic training in self-hypnosis, yoga biofeedback, transcendental meditation (TM), zazen, creative imagery, movement, exercise and breathing techniques. Learn about them and then make them part of your life – and, most important of all, enjoy doing them. Of course, they are doing you good and you should do what does you good, but they can also be a lot of fun. And no matter who you are, they can lead you into realms of awareness you have never lived in before, literally opening up whole new worlds of possibilities in your life, your relationships and your work.

THROW OUT THE CHRONIC STRESSORS

Every stressor – every situation that triggers off the stress response in you – is like a challenge. And one way of dealing effectively with long-term stress is to take a good look at what continues to trigger the stress response in you and to ask yourself the question, 'Is this particular thing a challenge I really want to meet, or is it something I would be better off eliminating from my life?' The question is an important one. Many stressors provide challenges from which one can grow, but some are simply habitual, rather like the treadmill in a hamster's cage. They lead you nowhere and they bring you little in terms of increasing awareness or an ability to make better use of your life and energies. If they are habitual stressors in your life, then consider eliminating them.

For instance, take a look at the work you do and ask whether it is really satisfying to you. What about the financial demands you have taken on – are they really necessary? If so, is there a way you haven't thought of to reduce them? If not, have the courage to drop them and accept the changes which doing so will bring about. We all have a tendency to hang on to the status quo at all costs – and usually the cost is at the loss of a lot of energy and life. Even if you learn the finest techniques for meditation and stilling the mind, if you are in a job year after year which you hate, or if you are faced with a relationship that no longer has meaning for you, they will all do little good. For while they may protect you from serious illness, you will still be banging your head against a brick wall. It is not only important to take responsibility for facing up to the demands of stress instead of trying to avoid it, is is also important to take responsibility for removing stress where it is no longer useful and relevant to you.

When stress needs to go
Stress can be a challenge. Accepting it, fighting it and winning can be a positive factor in your own personal growth. On the other hand, you may find you are subjecting yourself to habitual stress of a very negative kind – and this is the kind of stress that you need to eliminate from your life. Yoga and meditation can be a great help, but they won't cure all your troubles if you're in a job you hate. What they will do is to refresh you for a busy, active life that you enjoy.

PRINCIPLES OF RELAXATION

We live in a world of constant activity. It is a world of striving and goals, of planning and remembering – a world of never-ending sensory stimulation, of exciting new ideas and discoveries. Yet amidst all this activity somewhere inside you is a centre of stillness – a wordless, formless space where the seeds of creativity are sown that later become your ideas and your accomplishments. Here in the silence and the darkness you can hear your own 'inner voice'. You can come to know the difference between what you really want, feel and think, and what has been programmed into you by habits, false notions, and values that are not your own. This space, a woman's centre, is also a place of safety and security for her; she can move out of it as she chooses, to meet the outside world, to form friendships, to love and to learn. It is a permanent sanctuary to which she can return when she feels overburdened, tired, confused, or in need of new vitality and direction.

Locating this centre within yourself, recognizing its value, and then living your life more and more from it are an essential part of staying well and being beautiful – in short, of becoming what you are. The key that opens this particular door for most people is relaxation.

Find your inner voice
In a world of hectic activity, it is essential to keep contact with a centre of stillness inside yourself, to which you can retreat when the sensory bombardment from all around gets just too much. In this core of inner silence the only voice you will hear is your own. Listening to your own feelings and being in tune with yourself is the key to staying well and being beautiful, the key that will unlock the door to positive relaxation.

PASSIVE AWARENESS

By relaxation, I don't mean sleeping or flopping down on a bed when you feel you can't go on, or losing yourself in a mindless state in front of the television – although sleep is certainly essential and the other two states have many things to recommend them too. I mean something more: learning to move at will into a temporary state of deep stillness or meditation in which your usual concerns, your habitual thoughts, and the never-ending activity of your daily life are replaced by a kind of alert, yet totally passive, awareness. The relaxed state permits some of the physiological changes normally experienced during sleep to take place to revitalize your body and mind simultaneously. But it is different from sleep. For while your body is deeply passive, your mind is very alert.

For some people this state occurs spontaneously, often between sleep and wakefulness. It is then that their best ideas come or that they experience a sense of harmony in themselves and in relation to the rest of the world. Scientists studying this state of psychophysical relaxation find that the brain wave patterns in it are very different from those of the normally awake state. After tens of thousands of hours of observation of the changes in brain wave patterns in subjects hooked up to EEG equipment, researchers have been able to analyse and describe a number of interesting altered states of consciousness during relaxation, each with its own brain wave patterns, objective physical manifestations, and subjective feelings. They have discovered that there is an increase in overall awareness and creativity as a person moves from one level of relaxation into the next deeper one.

This is interesting, for most people have a fear of letting go, thinking that if they give up control of things they won't be able to think clearly or independantly or work well, or that someone is likely to put something over on them. In fact, just the opposite is true. When you are able to enter a state of deep relaxation at will, this frees you from patterns of living and thinking to which you tend to be a slave (although sometimes an unconscious one). It enables you to think more clearly and simply and to act more directly when action is called for. In other words, by establishing a purposeful pattern of this kind, you can mobilize your inner resources as and when you need them.

RELIEF FROM STRESS

Relaxation is also the most important key to freedom from the damaging effects of long-term stress. This is something which by now has been well established scientifically. Many studies have been made of people taught a relaxation technique and then monitored as to the psychological and physiological changes that take place after fifteen or twenty minutes of practising it. These studies show that relaxation techniques bring the parasympathetic branch of the autonomic nervous system into play, calming you, reducing oxygen consumption, lowering blood lactates (high lactate levels are associated with anxiety, arousal, and hypertension), slowing your heartbeat significantly, and changing brain wave patterns. They have also shown that repeated practice can lead to improved memory, increased perceptual ability, and a subjective feeling in participants that their work and their lives are somehow more creative than they were before.

Another interesting benefit from the daily practice of deep relaxation is a reduction of negative habit patterns such as drug taking (of both prescription and mind-altering drugs), alcohol consumption, and cigarette smoking. For instance, research in the United States involving 2,000 students between the ages of nineteen and twenty-three who had practised a form of meditation for periods of from a few months to a couple of years showed that their dependence on alcohol, drugs and cigarettes dropped sharply. The number of smokers was reduced by half in the first six months of doing the practice. By twenty-one months it was down to one third. And these changes were entirely spontaneous – at no time was any suggestion made that relaxation or meditation would change any of these habits.

Cardiologist Herbert Benson did the first studies into the effects of Transcendental Meditation with Keith Wallace many years ago at Harvard, then continued on his own to investigate this state of relaxation. He believes that each of us has what he calls the 'relaxation response' – a natural ability to experience the relaxed state with all its benefits – and that all we need to bring it about is some kind of tool to turn it on.

The possible tools are many. They range from transcendental meditation, yoga, breathing exercises, zazen, silent repetition of a word, and autogenic training to long-term strenuous exercise and biofeedback – the list is almost endless. Each can be useful as a tool for silencing everyday thoughts and for temporarily shutting off habitual ways of seeing the world and doing things – for creating a pathway between your inner and outer world. All of them are different, and for you some will work better or be more enjoyable than others. That is why it is worthwhile to try a few different techniques until you discover which ones you prefer.

Practising one or two techniques every day will make you aware of the enormous power your own mind has – power to alleviate suffering and bring a sense of well-being, power to change those things you want to change but which seemed impossible to change before, power to expand your whole awareness of your world of work, pleasure and relationships. Meanwhile, almost automatically you will reap the well-documented physical and psychological benefits of stilling your mind. But regular practice is important.

DISCIPLINE FOR FREEDOM

We live in an age where discipline is often looked down upon as something that impedes spontaneity and freedom, something old fashioned and stifling to life. We all tend to rebel against it. But it has been my experience, and the experience of a great many professionals working in the field of humanistic in-depth psychology, that the kind of discipline needed for daily practice of meditation or deep relaxation tends not to stifle one's ability to be involved in the spontaneous business of life but to free it. This is something you will have to find out for yourself. At first it may take a little effort to get up the fifteen minutes earlier each morning to practise a technique and to take fifteen minutes out of your busy afternoon or early evening to practise again, but you will find it is well worth it. The most common excuse is that you don't have time. The reality of the situation is that twice a day for fifteen to twenty minutes will give you time not take it from you, for you will find that you do everything with greater efficiency and enjoyment, that far less of your energy is wasted in fruitless activity. Every minute you spend in a deeply relaxed state will yield a fourfold return in the energy you need in your outer life.

Here are a few useful techniques to try. Some are

orientated more towards the body, such as Jacobson's progressive relaxation and many of the breathing techniques in the next chapter; others, such as Benson's relaxation response or zazen, focus more on the mental processes. But it is important to remember that there is no real separation between the two; mind and body are not different entities, they are merely different ends of the same continuum. Each technique affects both. It could not be otherwise.

PROGRESSIVE RELAXATION

A technique based on the work of Edmund Jacobson, this is an excellent way to begin if you have never done any sort of relaxation or meditation technique before, because it gives most people some sense of what relaxation feels like even the first time you try it. As you repeat your technique over and over again (it is best done for fifteen minutes at least twice a day), you will find you enter a state of relaxation that is progressively deeper and deeper.

You might find it helpful to have the instructions read to you by a friend, at least until you get to know them yourself, or to make a cassette recording of them to play while you are relaxing. Remember to leave enough time after each instruction for you to carry it out. The whole practice demands about fifteen minutes with a break of from two to five minutes while you experience the relaxed state you have achieved.

The first few times you try the technique, you may find you have trouble picturing all the images as they come or preventing your mind from wandering. It doesn't matter if you don't 'see' anything – some people are more visual in their imagery and others more feeling; both work superbly well – just approach the exercise from your own point of view. When you find your mind wandering (this is a common occurence because your concentration is not used to focusing so intensely, or because you are experiencing something new to you, which naturally enough causes a little anxiety) ask yourself 'why is my mind wandering?' Pursue that thought for a couple of minutes, then go back to the exercise and continue to go through it as best you can. All difficulties will iron themselves out automatically after you have practised the technique long enough – so persevere to overcome any initial difficulties.

PRINCIPLES OF RELAXATION

1. Find a quiet room, preferably one without too much light, and sit in a comfortable chair that gives support to your back. Place both feet flat on the floor and close your eyes.

2.Become aware of your breathing and just let the air come in and out of your body without doing anything.

3. Take a few deep breaths. Each time you breathe out, slowly repeat the word 'relax' silently to yourself.

4. Focus on your face and let yourself feel any tension in your face or eyes, your jaw or tongue. Make a mental picture of tension – you could picture a clenched fist, a knotted rope, or a hard ball of steel – then mentally picture the tension going and everything becoming relaxed, like a limp rubber band.

5. Feel your face and your eyes, your jaw and your tongue becoming relaxed, and as they relax, experience a wave of relaxation spreading through your whole body. (Each step takes about ten seconds)

6. Tighten up all the muscles in your face and eyes, squeezing them as hard as you can. Then let go and feel the relaxation spread throughout your body again.

7. Now apply the same instruction to other parts of your body, moving slowly downwards from your head to your neck, shoulders, and upper back, arms, hands, chest, mid-and lower back, your abdomen, thighs and calves, ankles, feet and toes, going through each area until every part of your body is relaxed. With each part, picture the tension in it mentally and then picture it going away; each time, tense the muscles in that area and then let them go and feel the relaxation spreading.

8. When you've relaxed every part of your body, sit quietly in this comfortable state for up to five minutes.

9. Now let the muscles in your eyelids become lighter ... get ready to open your eyes and come back to an awareness of the room.

10. Open your eyes. Now you are ready to go about whatever you want to do.

Progressive relaxation
Sitting in a quiet room by
yourself, you can be aware
of the rhythm of your
breathing. By concentrating
on images of tension – such
as a clenched fist – and then
imagining the tension
flooding from them, you will
gradually feel waves of
relaxation spread over your
whole body.

ZAZEN

One of the simplest ways of meditating, this technique involves nothing more than just being aware of your breathing. But don't be deceived by its simplicity. It is a potent tool for stilling the mind and regenerating the body. And concentrating your awareness on the breath is not as easy as it sounds. It needs thinking about exactly what you are intending to achieve.

1. Find yourself a quiet place where you will not be disturbed. You can sit cross-legged on the floor with a small cushion underneath you or you can sit in a chair if you prefer, but your back should be straight. (This straight-back position is a requirement for many meditation techniques since it creates a physical equilibrium which makes calm mental focus possible.) Let your hands rest quietly on your lap.

2. Close your eyes. Take several long, slow breaths, breathing from your abdomen so it swells out with each in breath and sinks in again when you breathe out.

3. Now rock your body from side to side and then around in large, gentle circles from your hips to the top of your head. Rock in increasingly smaller circles until you gradually come to rest in the centre.

4. Now breathe in and out through your nose quietly without doing anything to your breathing (that is, don't try to breathe deeper or slower or faster; just breathe normally). With each out breath, count silently to yourself. So it goes: in breath, out breath, 'one'; in breath, out breath, 'two'; and so on up to ten, counting only on the out breath. When you get to ten go back and begin again at one. If you lose count halfway, it doesn't matter. Go back and start the count at one again. Counting isn't the whole point, but only a tool for focusing your mind on your breath.

If you are like most people, the first few times you do the exercise you will find you lose count often and you are often distracted by thoughts or noises. Each time some random thought distracts you, simply turn your mind gently back again to counting the breaths. Distractions don't change the effectiveness of the meditation.

5. After fifteen minutes (sneak a look at your wristwatch if you must), stop. Sit still for a moment, then open your eyes and slowly begin to go about your everyday activities again.

This exercise, like most techniques, is best done twice a day, morning and evening. A beginner will usually notice positive results by the end of the week but they become increasingly apparent the longer you go on doing it. Some Buddhist monks do this exercise for two or three years before beginning any other form of meditation.

Breath – a potent tool
Breathing is something we never normally think about, yet concentrating on nothing but drawing breath and letting it gently out of your body again is a potent way of stilling your mind and regenerating your resources. Practising zazen twice a day will bring almost immediate benefits, and the longer you continue with it, the greater these will be.

BENSON'S RELAXATION RESPONSE TECHNIQUE

Herbert Benson, who wrote The Relaxation Response, discovered that the same measurable physical benefits that accrue from practising Transcendental Meditation, which depends on the silent repetition of a mantra (a word sound), can be had by repeating any word over and over while the eyes are closed and the body is in a quiet state.

Meditation by concentration on a mantra or word sound has a long tradition. Some mantras are said to be sacred words that have particular sound vibrations which transmit particular powers. Each tradition has its own mantras such as Guru Om, Om mani padme hum, La ilaha illa 'Ilah, or in the Catholic faith, 'Hail Mary, full of grace, the Lord is with thee'. Whether their magic aspects are true or not, the technique works beautifully to replace the habitual chatter that runs through one's mind, such as worries about things past and things yet to come.

Benson suggests you find a word that is pleasing to you. It could be anything – say, 'flower', 'peace', or 'love'. He likes the word 'one' as it is simple and has the connotation of unity about it. (The teacher Krishnamurti once remarked that any word would be better than the fruitless and often destructive thoughts that normally run through our minds; then he wryly suggested 'Coca-Cola'). Here's how you go about practising this technique.

1. Find a quiet place where you won't be disturbed for fifteen to twenty minutes and a comfortable chair that supports your back.

2. Sit down and close your eyes. Give yourself a moment to settle in and you are ready to begin.

3. Simply sit there, feet on the floor and eyes closed, quietly repeating your word over and over to yourself: 'one...one...one...'

4. Whenever your mind wanders or you are disturbed by a sound or thought, simply turn your mind gently back to repeating the word again.

5. That is all there is to it. After fifteen to twenty minutes stop repeating the mantra and get ready to open your eyes.

Meditation and the mantra
A mantra is simply a word of your choice - one that you like - which you repeat over and over again to yourself to clear your mind of the habitual chatter that runs through it. This simple process prepares you for meditation. It also enables you to return refreshed to your everyday activities.

6. Open your eyes, stretch, and go about your everyday activities. This is a particularly useful technique once you have practised it a few times because you can do it in so many different places, such as in a waiting room or on a commuter train or bus. I know a lot of men and women who have made it part of their daily trek to and from work with tremendous benefits.

TOTAL BODY RELAXATION

Like Jacobson's progressive relaxation, this technique is useful for getting rid of physical tension rapidly as well as in preparation for using creative imagery. It is also a technique that is often used in self-hypnosis. Unlike many relaxation or meditation exercises, it is often done lying down. Once you get the hang of it and have done it a few times, it becomes so efficient that the whole process from alert wakefulness to deep relaxation can demand no more than a couple of minutes. This is hard to believe at the beginning, but it is so. I have used it for years in bed each morning before I get up and each evening before I go to sleep, together with imagery or visualization about things I want to

From tip to toe A very good way of totally relaxing the body from tip to toe is to concentrate on each part of it in turn, telling all the tension to flood from it, feeling your limbs lying warm and heavy, pressing into the softness of the pillow on which you are lying.

change in my life. I also use it in the middle of the night if ever I am awakened instead of just lying in bed fitfully trying to go back to sleep again.

If you do it during the day, it is often useful to place a small pillow under your knees while you lie back, your arms quietly at your sides or folded over your abdomen. If you like you can put the directions on tape for use until you have mastered the technique.

1. Lie down in a quiet, preferably dark room. Get comfortable with a pillow or two under your head and one under your knees too if you wish. Now close your eyes and take a few deep breaths, letting them out completely before you begin.

2. Think of your feet. Forget everything else and just concentrate on your feet. Now mentally tell them to let go; say to yourself silently, 'My feet are relaxing and getting heavy – heavy and warm, warm and relaxed. They are sinking into the bed.'

3. Now go to your ankles. 'My ankles are getting heavier and heavier, more and more relaxed – relaxed and floppy, floppy and warm and heavy. I let them go completely.' Now go on to your calves and then to your thighs – 'my calves are getting heavier and heavier, warm and heavy, heavy and relaxed. They are sinking into the bed – heavy and relaxed, relaxed and floppy. I let them go completely.'

4. Now you give the same directions to each part of your body, moving from toes to head, one part to the next part, relaxing each part as you go – hips, back ('I let go vertebra by vertebra all the way up my spine') – then come around to the front, to the abdomen ('My tummy is warm and relaxed, all soft and floppy, sinking heavily into the bed'). Then chest, neck, shoulders, head, face, tongue, jaw and eyes. Now do your arms, forearms, hands and fingers, until every part of your body is given the direction to let go. 'My whole body is completely still...warm and relaxed...heavy...quiet and at peace...relaxed and warm. I can feel it in my mind.'

Now you are ready to use whatever visualization you want or you can let yourself sink even deeper into relaxation by counting backwards from ten to one, saying with each number, 'I am sinking deeper and deeper into a state of warm relaxation...deeper and deeper.' When you reach 'one', stay for a few minutes in this peaceful, relaxed state, feeling the calm all through you. Then, when you are ready to finish say to yourself, 'Now I am going to open my eyes and get up feeling pleasantly fresh and well.' Open your eyes and get up.

This exercise is done entirely in the mind. No physical movements are necessary as you go through the body. You are telling your body to let go. That is one of the reasons it is useful for making you aware of how much of an effect your mind can exert over your body. When you begin to practise, don't be discouraged if you feel you are not very relaxed sometimes – it works even so, and the more you practise the easier it will become. After having practised it a few times you will feel the pleasant warmth and tingling of the relaxation. Don't try to do anything – just let it happen.

BEYOND RELAXATION

Once you are familiar with the practice of deep relaxation or meditation and with all the benefits it can bring you, you might be interested to go on to investigate other, more complex forms of meditation. There are many, for meditation is not a word that is easy to define. It takes in such different practices. Some forms such as zazen or vispassana (sometimes called insight meditation) demand complete immobility. You sit watching the rise and fall of your abdomen as you breathe, and when ever your mind wanders you gently turn it back to this observation. This simply concentrated attention, which can be likened to the 'continuum of awareness' in Gestalt theory, is capable of bringing up many repressed feelings and thoughts that have been stifling your full expression and of liberating them. The Siddha Yoga of Muktananda and the chaotic meditation of Rajneesh where the body is let go to move as it will, are examples of this sort. They often involve spontaneous changes in muscle tension and relaxation and in breathing, and they demand a sense of surrender to the physical body for the release of the mental, emotional and bodily tensions. These kinds of meditation can be particularly good for someone with a tendancy to be physically rigid.

Then there are the visualization meditations such as those used in Tibetan Buddhism in which you focus your mind on a particular image, fine-tuning it to the specific beneficial energies or influences this symbol carries (the creative imagery techniques in the next chapter are also an example of this kind of meditation). They have been used recently to cure serious illness and also in the sports world to improve athletic performance. Another form of meditation is that of 'mindfulness', where you go about your daily activities simply being aware of each thing you do, as in Gurdjieff's 'self-remembering', shikantaza or mahamudra. These are just a few of the possibilities worth investigating if you want to go further. Each has something worthwhile to offer and the mere act of learning a new method and the set of ideas and attitudes that go with it can be an exciting experience as well as tremendously beneficial.

UNDERSTANDING SLEEP

Sleep is a healer. It regenerates your body, rejuvenates your skin, clears emotional conflicts, and helps you think and work at top efficiency. It is another form of relaxation essential to health and beauty. In many ways, though, sleep remains a mystery in spite of all the elaborate research that has been done into how and why we sleep and dream.

Most of the common notions about sleep are untrue. For instance, sleep is not some kind of 'little death' from which you are rescued every morning. Nor do you go to bed to fall deeper and deeper into sleep until you reach bottom sometime after midnight, after which you come closer and closer to consciousness until you finally awaken. Also, deep sleep is not any more beneficial than light sleep. And we do not necessarily need the obligatory eight hours a night to remain well and fresh-looking.

THE TWO FACES OF SLEEP

There are two kinds of sleep; orthodox sleep, which is dreamless – sometimes called 'synchronized slow wave sleep' (S) because of the brain patterns that accompany it – and is vital for physical restoration of the body, and paradoxical sleep, during which dreaming occurs along with rapid eye movement (REM) – sometimes called desynchronized sleep (D) – and which is essential to your mental and emotional stability. Research into sleep measured by electroencephalographs has shown that all of us spend our sleep time in and out of the two stages in a predictable rhythmic pattern. If for any reason this pattern is repeatedly disturbed, we suffer.

There are four levels or depths of orthodox sleep. When you fall asleep you move into the first level, characterized by low-amplitude fast-frequency brain wave patterns. (Sometimes sleep starts with a sudden twitching movement that is called a myoclonic jerk. This is the result of a sudden flare-up of electrical activity in the brain, as in a minor epileptic seizure). Then, as you move to level two and even deeper into levels three and four, there is a general slowing of the frequency and an increase in the amplitude of your brain waves. All through each night you move in and out of these levels in your own characteristic pattern.

Normally one falls off to sleep and remains for a short time at level one and two and then plunges into levels three or four to stay there for seventy to one hundred minutes. At that point comes the first period of REM or paradoxical sleep when dreams begin. This dream period of REM lasts only ten to twenty minutes. It is repeated again at about ninety minute intervals throughout the night, with orthodox – undreaming sleep – in between.

During orthodox sleep your body is quiet. Heartbeat slows down, blood pressure falls slightly, and your breathing gets slower and more regular. Even your digestive system slows down. In the deeper levels of orthodox sleep, brain waves gradually become more synchronized, as if everything in your body is at peace. During these times, your body's restorative processes come into their own, rapidly repairing damaged tissues and cells, producing antibodies to fight infection, and carrying out a myriad of other duties necessary to keep you healthy. Without orthodox sleep in all its different stages, this important vegetative restoration does not take place properly and you become more prone to illness, early ageing, fatigue and muddled thinking. Orthodox sleep is the master restorer.

REM sleep, which is diametrically opposite to orthodox sleep in many ways, is just as vital. It more than earns its name 'paradoxical' by being a mass of contradictions: although the body is virtually paralyzed during the REM state, the fingers and the face often twitch and the genitals become erect. Breathing speeds up to the level of your normal waking state. Heartbeat rate, blood pressure aand temperature rise and adrenalin shoots through the system. Beneath the lids, eyes move more rapidly from side to side as though you were watching a film or a tennis match. And this is exactly what is happening

Sleep and dreaming

Research into sleep and dreaming has shown that there are two types of sleep – orthodox sleep, which is vital for physical restoration and paradoxical sleep, during which we dream. The latter is vital for our mental and emotional stability.

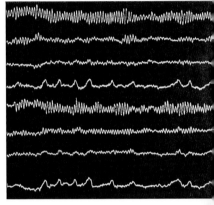

Sleep patterns

This electroencephalograph reading shows the relaxed patterns of deep sleep. This is not a constant state, since the brain is always active. If you are stressed, the pattern will probably be more irregular.

– you are viewing images that come rapidly in succession. Your brain waves in the REM state show a marked similarity to the rapid, irregular patterns of being awake.

The first REM period of dreaming usually happens after you have been asleep for ninety minutes and lasts for about ten minutes. After that they occur regularly throughout the night, culminating in the longest period (usually about half an hour) just before you wake up.

WHY WE DREAM

Although the exact purpose of REM sleep remains somewhat a mystery, researchers know that it is essential for maintaining one's mental and emotional equilibrium. The need for paradoxical sleep also varies from one person to another. How much you will need is related both to your personality and psychological state. Longer and more frequent periods of REM sleep take place in times of psychic pain, or when your defence patterns are being challenged by new demands. Women tend to have increased REM periods during the premenstrum – the three or four days before the beginning of a period. For most women this is a time of increased anxiety, irritability, mood changes and unstable defence patterns.

But there is a lot that is still not known about the function of paradoxical sleep. Well-known French researcher Michel Jouvet, who has done extensive studies of the REM state in animals and their unborn young (in which it occurs as well), believes it is a kind of practice of genetic code in which lower animals run through their instinctive behaviour patterns. In mammals and man, he thinks, it is a time when we are probably practising our learned behaviour as each night we go through the process of integrating new information with the knowledge we already have.

When animals are deprived of REM sleep they become increasingly excitable, appetite soars, a perverted sexuality appears, and eventually they suffer a nervous breakdown. So far, studies show that too little REM makes them more and more restless and anxious. Their short-term memory starts to fail and they suffer from poor concentration and other unpleasant symptoms. Sleep researchers have discovered this by watching carefully, and each time subjects enter the paradoxical stage of sleep (indicated by rapid eye movements clearly visible beneath the lids), they awaken them.

This aspect of REM sleep is particularly interesting, for when scientists disturbed sleepers in the orthodox state, they found that deprivation of orthodox sleep doesn't lead to any psychological disturbances. But after being deprived of REM sleep for several days, sleepers became desperate for it. Their normal sleep patterns alter so that they slip into REM immediately on falling asleep and then experience twenty to thirty periods of it each night instead of the usual three. Psychologists refer to this phenomenon as 'REM rebound'. It is often accompanied by fierce nightmares as psychic imagery, too long repressed, seeks strongly to reassert itself.

BEWARE OF SLEEPING PILLS

Sleeping pills repress the REM stage and repression may result in lasting psychological damage to any pill popper. After taking sleep-inducing drugs regularly, when you come off them you may fear you are going mad as you start to experience REM rebound. Vivid and frightening hypnagocic images and nightmares appear as the body hungrily tries to make up for what it has been denied.

There are other reasons to steer clear of sleep-inducing drugs. Both barbiturates and nonbarbiturates prescribed for sleep are physically and psychologically addictive (barbiturates to an even greater degree than heroin). They can also be fatal, even at a low dosage, when mixed with alcohol in the bloodstream. Finally – something that few people realize – they are not very effective over the long term. Sleeping pills can be successfully used to bring on sleep only for the first week or two. After that dangerously increased doses are needed.

For many women who rely on sleeping pills, the power of suggestion brought about by putting one in the mouth and swallowing it is far more useful than the drug in inducing sleep. The drug itself can only do harm, in the long run. There are other, safer and more effective ways of getting to sleep.

HOW MUCH SLEEP DO YOU NEED

The amount of sleep you need varies tremendously from one woman to another. It also varies from one day to the next. There is no truth in the idea that you need eight hours of sleep to stay well and feel energetic. You might need ten hours while another woman gets on very well with four and a half. One study showed that short sleepers tend to be active, outgoing people who are sociable, flexible in their personalities, and more conformist socially. Those wanting longer periods of sleep are more introverted and creative and are particularly good at sustained work. Often the more stress-filled your day, the more sleep you will need to recover from it.

As people get older they tend to sleep less. Many sixty and seventy year olds get by on a mere three or four hours a day. Occasionally you meet someone who sleeps as little as half an hour to an hour each night, yet appear to be perfectly normal. The amount of sleep you need depends so much on your biological and psychological individuality that you can't make hard and fast rules about it. Many high achievers and great minds throughout history – Napoleon, Freud and Thomas Eddison, for instance – have been poor sleepers while others like Einstein could sleep the day away.

But the idea that you need a certain amount of sleep each night to stay well is a powerful one. For many people it is so embedded in their unconscious that if they get only seven hours one night instead of eight, they are convinced they will be tired the next day and soon develop all the signs of it. If you are one of these people, try re-examining your premises and experiment – sleep less and see what happens. You may find that how you feel after a certain amount of sleep depends more on your attitude than on the time spent in bed. Try sleeping less for a few days; many women find that, when they do, they actually have more energy.

STOP WORRYING ABOUT INSOMNIA

A lot of so-called insomnia is nothing more than the result of worrying about getting to sleep. Many people who consider themselves insomniacs are really victims of general propaganda about sleep rather than non-sleepers. Many women seek treatment because they can only sleep four or five hours a night, although that may be all they need. There is nothing more apt to cause sleeplessness than the worry that you won't be able to drop off. Sometimes, too, sleeplessness is normal. After all, we all experience a sleepless night now and then, particularly if we are overtired, worried or excited about some coming event.

Real chronic insomnia is less frequent. A major research project into long-term insomnia turned up some interesting facts about sufferers. Over 85 percent of the insomniacs studied had one or more major pathological personality indications, such as depression, obsessive compulsive tendencies, schizophrenic characteristics or sociopathy. For them, their insomnia was a secondary symptom of a more basic conflict; it was a socially acceptable problem they could talk about without fear of being judged harshly. Insomnia like this is little more than a mask for whatever underlying problem is really bothering the non-sleeper.

Occasionally, the inability to sleep can be a manifestation of a nutritional problem – often a deficiency of zinc coupled with an excess of copper, which produces a mind that is overactive intellectually and won't wind down – or a deficiency of calcium or vitamin E, which can lead to tension and cramping in the muscles and a difficulty in letting go.

The more easy-going an attitude you take to sleep, the less likely you are to have a problem with it. If you miss an hour or two, or if you are not sleepy, simply stay up, read a book or finish some work. Believe it or not, one of the best times for coming up with creative ideas is in the middle a sleepless night. And chances are that you'll more than make up for it in the next couple of days – provided you don't get anxious about it.

HOW – AND HOW NOT – TO GET TO SLEEP

1. Get more exercise regularly during the day. This helps burn up stress-caused adrenalin building up in the brain, which can result in that tense, nervous feeling when you're 'up' and you can't seem to get 'down'. But don't take strenuous exercise before going to bed, as it can set the heart pounding and stimulate the whole body too much.

2. Don't go to bed when you are not sleepy. Instead pursue some pleasant activity, preferably passive. Television is not the best choice, for rays emitted from the set disturb your nervous system when you least need it.

3. Don't drink coffee, alcohol, or strong stimulants at dinner. This isn't just an old wive's tale. One researcher looking into the effects of caffeine on human beings recently showed that total sleep time is decreased by two hours and the mean total of intervening wakefulness more than doubles when patients are given three milligrams of caffeine, the equivalent of a couple of cups of coffee. Alcohol may put you to sleep but it tends not to keep you there, awakening you instead in the early hours.

4. Don't let anyone smoke in your bedroom. Stuffy air can prevent you from sleeping.

5. Stop worrying about getting to sleep. Just let it happen. If it doesn't tonight, so what? It will tomorrow night, or the next. Lack of sleep is not going to kill you, but worrying about it long enough just might.

NATURE'S SLEEP AIDS

1. Milk. It is an old fashioned remedy, maybe, but it is scientifically sound that drinking a glass of milk before bed helps you sleep. Milk contains trytophan, an amino acid that is converted in the body to serotonin, a brain chemical that sets off the deeper levels of sleep. It is high in calcium and is often referred to as the slumber mineral because it induces muscle relaxation.

2. An ionizer. A little contraption beside your bed that sends negative ions into the air and is a God send to anyone who has the kind of nervous-system that tends to go 'up' and doesn't want to come 'down'. Although not cheap, it is an excellent investment, for you can use it at a desk when you have a lot of work to do. Or, if you buy one of the portable varieties, you can also take it in the car on long trips to keep from going to sleep (it magically works both ways) and on airplane trips to minimize the effects of jetlag. Negative ions also stimulate the production of serotonin in the brain.

3. Take a lukewarm bath, submerging yourself as much as possible for ten minutes. Then, wrapping a towel around you just long enough to get rid of the drips, pop into bed immediately. Lukewarm water is the most relaxing of all temperatures on the body. A hot bath before bed is a mistake. It is far too stimulating to the heart and gets your motor running.

4. Get into a rut! Going to bed as far as possible at the same time every night and developing a routine or simple ritual about it. Doing the same thing every night before bed quickly accustoms the mind to accept sleep.

5. Practise a relaxation or mediation technique twice a day. A valuable tool for insomnia, it will lower

Sleeping aids Avoid man-made sleeping aids, if you can – they will not help you in the long term. Natural tranquilizers, such as a refreshing herbal tea, are much more of a help, especially when combined with other herbal soothers.

elevated blood pressure and help you to cope better with whatever stress you tend to carry off to bed with you.

6. Get to know the natural tranquillizers and herb teas and use them whenever you feel the need, sweetened with honey if you like, as a bedtime drink. Peppermint, camomile, skullcap, catnip and vervain are renowned for their relaxing effects. Or you can try some passiflora (passionflower), which is probably the best-known of the herbal soothers. Many health food stores carry it in tablet form.

THE BREATH OF VITALITY

Even more important than the food you eat is the air you breathe and the way you breathe it. They can affect how you feel emotionally and physically, how your skin looks (for cells of the skin are dependent for their metabolic processes on a constant supply of enough oxygen), how much vitality you have, and even how clearly you can think.

Because breathing is the only one of your body's functions that can either be completely involuntary or voluntary, it can form a bridge between your conscious and unconscious functions. This makes it possible to look at your breathing to find out how you are feeling and what is happening to your body. It also means that you can use breathing to change your energy level or your mood.

BREATH ENERGY

Throughout history the breath has been associated with energy, force and power of both a physical and a metaphysical kind. In the Bible, the word translated as 'spirit' can also be translated as 'air'. It is the invisible life force, the energy the Chinese call 'chi' and attempt to manipulate in acupuncture treatments. The Sufis refer to it as 'baraks'. It plays an important role in their techniques of meditation. The yogis call it 'Prana' and claim it is responsible for the extraordinary control they can exert over their mind and bodies. Prana means breath, respiration, life, vitality, wind, energy and strength. It is also used to mean soul as distinguished from body. Yogis believe that if we are able to control our breath we can also control pain, emotions and physical health, as well as supernatural phenomena.

THE BODY'S CLEARING SYSTEM

While the act of breathing is supplying your cells with the oxygen they need, it is also removing carbon dioxide and wastes from your system. Carbon dioxide is a by-product of oxidation and energy release. If it were allowed to build up it would poison the cells and eventually kill them. So tiny vessels carry the waste back to the lungs, where

THE AIR WE BREATHE

The air you breathe is not a chemical compound but a simple mixture of gases: Earth's atmosphere contains four times as much nitrogen as it does oxygen, together with 0.03 percent carbon dioxide and minute amounts of other rare gases. Its carbonic acid content varies between 0.02 percent and 0.06 percent (when it is higher, the oxygen content is lower). In addition, it contains traces of water – in the form of water vapour – a little ammonia, various mineral salts and ozone. This curious mixture is the most necessary stuff in the world for all forms of life. You can live only a few minutes without air.

We tend to think that the energy we have comes from the food we eat. But as the ancient traditions teach, air, not food, is the primary fuel for driving the human engine. Without the oxygen air contains, your body would not be able to break down the nutrients you take in through your foods in order to produce energy and nourish your cells. When air is first taken into the lungs, it fills the tiny bronchioles. Oxygen diffuses through their membranes into your bloodstream and is carried throughout your body to every cell of every organ and tissue. Your blood is capable of absorbing up to four times as much oxygen as water can, as long as there is enough iron available to produce haemoglobin, which carries the oxygen through the bloodstream. One of the most important common symptoms of iron deficiency – anaemia – is the inability to catch your breathe – you simply cannot get enough oxygen.

it is eliminated when you breathe out and exchanged for new oxygen when you breathe in. At least that is how it should work.

In most women, however, this vital process of taking in necessary oxygen and eliminating poisonous wastes is neither as efficient nor as complete as it should be. This can be due to many things, from tissue anoxia as a result of a diet too high in fats, to insufficient iron, B12 folic acid, or vitamin E resulting in anaemia. But by far the most common cause is simply poor breathing. Most of us use only half our breathing potential and we expel only half the wastes, so in effect we are only getting from oxygen half the support for health and beauty that we should be getting. And because we don't exhale fully, when we take in new air the old air that is still in the lungs is sucked deeper into the sacs. This means that the oxygen level in the tiny alveoli which supply the body, is far lower than it would be if the air contained were fresh from the outside. Thus the amount of oxygen available to the blood, brain and nerves, as well as the skin and the rest of the body, is reduced.

From the point of view of skin health and beauty alone, this can matter a lot. Seven percent of the oxygen you take in is used directly by your skin. When skin cells don't get all the oxygen they need, they are unable to carry out cell division rapidly and efficiently and the elimination of wastes is impeded, which contributes to more rapid ageing of the tissues.

Less than optimum levels of oxygen in your body can also effect the brain and nerve cells. In fact, there is considerable evidence that many of the mental changes usually associated with old age, such as senility and vagueness of thought, as well as certain physical illnesses are the result of too little oxygen being available to the cells, either as a result of limited breathing or blockages in the circulatory system, or both. Hyperbaric oxygen therapy, which involves giving pressurized and concentrated oxygen, has recently been used experimentally to treat a variety of ailments from osteomyelitis of the spine to brain damage.

Some researchers also believe that the air we breathe may at least be partly responsible for the subtle energy field which surrounds and pervades the bodies of humans and animals and which changes according to their state of health or disease.

On a more simple level some physicians and therapists such as the late Captain William P. Knowles have had excellent results when treating chronic chest complaints, fatigue, depression and nervous disorders simply by teaching patients the art of breathing fully. Making changes in the way you breathe or using specific methods of breath control can also help you do a lot of useful things such as increase your vitality, calm your emotions when they are disturbed, and clear an overtaxed mind.

THE BREATH OF EMOTION

The link between the way you breathe and your emotional state is well established. Not only do your emotions affect your breathing (remember the last time you were frightened and gasped for breath? how when you are excited your breathing becomes shallower and and faster than usual?), but how you breathe can bring in or turn off emotional states too. Here's an experiment that shows this: start to breathe very shallowly so only the shoulders and top of the chest show any signs of movement, and pant in and out very quickly for about forty-five seconds. At the end of that time your heart will be pounding and you will have all the feelings of anxiety and fear. Or try it the other way round. The next time you are in a difficult situation and feel you might lose control, stop, take three or four long deep breaths from the abdomen and let them out slowly. Then take another look at the challenge. You'll find your mind and feelings a lot calmer.

The art of normal breathing is something I think every woman concerned with protecting her good looks and preserving her health should know. When your lung capacity is developed and used to the full, you will have more energy, suffer less from fatigue, and be able to think more clearly. It will also make your skin glow with health and your eyes shine. And it is not as difficult as you might imagine. It involves no more than learning a few new habits. Let's look at four that you can start developing right now. Then we'll go on to some for specific effects.

THE ART OF FULL BREATHING

1. When you breathe, breathe with your whole chest and abdomen too. Most of us breathe only with the top part of our body, which means we are not fully lowering the diaphragm and expanding the lungs and so are not making use of their full capacity. This kind of restricted breathing stifles emotional expression and is often linked with anxiety, depression and worry. To check for abdominal breathing, put your hands on your tummy. Does it swell when you breathe in and sink when you breathe out? It should. Lying flat on a firm surface, practise breathing fully and gently until you get the feel of it.

2. Make sure that with each out breath you let out all the air you take in. By exhaling more of the carbon dioxide, you will get rid of more of the cells' waste products and you will be able to make full use of each new breath of air.

3. Take up some kind of aerobic exercise – such as running, bicycling or dancing – that demands full use of your lungs every day.

4. Use the following exercise for five minutes twice a day to increase your lung capacity, slim your middle, purify your blood, and help you to learn the art of fuller breathing. You can also use it whenever you feel tense or need to clear your head: Resting your hands on your rib cage at the sides, just above the waist, breathe out completely. Now inhale gently through the nose, letting your abdomen swell as much as it will to a slow count of five. Continue to breathe in through the nose to another count of five, this time letting your ribs expand under your hands and finally your chest too (but don't raise your shoulders in the process). Hold your breath for a count of five, now slowly let it out through your mouth as you count slowly to ten, noticing how your rib cage shrinks beneath your hands and pulling in with your abdomen until you have released all the air. Repeat four times.

Here are a few special breathing techniques for specific ends.

SENSUOUS BREATHING

This technique, taught to me by one of Britain's top biogenetic therapists, is a wonderful way of rediscovering the feel of your body. The therapist uses it to encourage the unblocking of any repressed emotional or physical tensions. She also claims that it increases one's ability to experience heightened sexual pleasure all over the body.

Lie on the floor on your back and relax as much as you can, letting your arms and legs flop. Close your eyes and feel your body against the floor; do you notice any tension in any part of it? Shoulders? Back? Legs? Now focus inside your body and ask yourself where you feel any movement in your muscles because of your breathing. Anywhere you feel tense, imagine your breathing into that spot, imagine you can exhale through that part of your body and as you do, experience the breath relaxing your sore muscles as it filters through them. Then, when you are relaxed, experiment with the movements which are part of natural, free breathing. They are beautiful movements.

When you breathe in, feel your pelvis tip back

Breath and energy
The air you breathe is even more important for health and vitality than the food you eat, yet most people hardly ever take a deep breath, so that their lungs only work at half power and oxygen circulation is minimal. Taking up a sport such as running.or cycling will tone up your body, expand your lungs and get your blood sparkling with oxygen. It's a wonderful way to start the day.

gently so there is slight arch to your back while your abdomen and chest rise, ribs and back expand, and chin tilts forward just barely. Then, when you exhale, your pelvis moves down again so your spine almost touches the floor, your back contracts, and your chin and head move back again exposing the front of your neck a bit more. This natural movement is a wave like motion that flows without hesitation from each in breath to its following out breath and so on. Practise it, exaggerating the tiny movements at first until you get the feel of it and then it will flow naturally.

THE DECANTER

This exercise stimulates the nervous system and at the same time stills a restless or anxious mind. I like doing it after I have been working in an immobile position for a long time – for instance, when I have been at my desk, writing for several hours. I do it just before I get up to move about.

Sitting comfortably in a chair with a straight back

or cross-legged on the floor, imagine that your body is like a decanter, the bottom of the decanter being your pelvis and hips and the top of it your head. Pretend that you are going to fill it with energy in the form of air. Now breathing in slowly, imagine it filling up gradually. After you have taken in as much air as you can comfortably hold and are getting to the top, hold your breath as long as necessary to become aware of a feeling of fullness. Then exhale slowly and imagine that it is emptying as you do. Repeat this five to ten times. (If you find yourself becoming light headed, it is nothing to worry about. This often happens if the lungs are not used to being fully used. But don't ever force your breathing.)

TENSION TAKER

This exercise is useful to do whenever you find yourself under stress or feel you are getting tense.

Stand comfortably with your arms at your sides and inhale through your nose slowly. Hunch up your shoulders as high as you can, clench your fists and, standing on tiptoes, tense your body harder and harder, concentrating on your centre – the navel area – to help keep your balance. Hold your breath and sink back onto your feet, loosening your shoulders and letting them drop. As you unclench your fists, exhale through your nose very slowly, pushing down through your palms and on your shoulders. Do this five or six times.

REVITALIZER

This exercise was taught to me by a friend who teaches yoga. It is wonderful if you are feeling drowsy from sitting too long or are very tired. It revitalizes you very quickly.

Let all the air out of your lungs – then even more – and then even more. Now take a deep breath from your abdomen so it swells as you breathe in. Exhale immediately through your nose, jerking in your abdomen momentarily and then jerk it in again, pushing out even more air. Repeat this five times until your lungs are completely empty. Now take in a long, slow breath, retain it for a count of five, and slowly exhale it all away. Repeat the whole exercise five times.

The revitalizer This is a breathing exercise you can do to wake up your senses after you have been sitting for a long time at a desk. It involves expelling every last puff of stale air from your body so that you can breathe freshly again.

PRANA POWER

This is an interesting exercise which makes use of the breath to do all sorts of surprising things such as banishing minor aches and pains caused by tension. If practised regularly it can also help keep the skin of your face looking smooth and wrinkle-free. It is a simple yogic technique for directing prana, or breath energy, to whatever part of your body needs it.

Sitting in a relaxed position with your spine firmly supported, or lying on a firm bed, slowly breathe in deeply, imagining the life force you are taking in as you do. Hold the breath for a few seconds... then, as you begin to breathe out, imagine directing the energy to whatever part of your body you want to affect for the better. For instance, see the skin on your face as soft and unlined and direct the energy there, or direct it at your shoulders to make them lose tension and so forth. Repeat the process for three to five minutes at a time. If you are using it for smoothing away lines on the face, you need to do it twice a day. It is good to do just after relaxation or meditation exercise if you can.

WHY YOGA

Like good breathing, yoga can also make you beautiful. And I don't mean by simply trimming a flabby thigh or flattening a neglected stomach. Of course, it will do these things too. But what I mean is more fundamental. The meaning of the word yoga is 'union,' or in more modern terms, 'integration.' Practising yoga regularly can bring a sense of calmness, poise, and detachment that eliminates the negative effects of stress and clears away tensions that stifle the full expression of your individuality – intellectually, emotionally, physically, and spiritually. It will help you to make the most of your life, however stressed you may be feeling.

You should not rush into any yoga programme; build up gradually and do not tackle exercises if your body tells you it is not up to them. And check with your doctor if you feel at all uncertain about their physical demands, particularly if you are ill, pregnant or suffering from muscle strain.

THE THREE SELVES

According to yogic theory, there are three basic levels or modes of expression in human life: the subconcious or instinctive self; the intellectual or reasoning self; and the mind from which intuition, inspiration, and real creativity spring. In order to be healthy on all levels, these three need to be balanced. In most of us they are not; one or another or even all three are underdeveloped, overactive, or uncontrolled. For instance, you've met the kind of person whose intellectual life is particularly vital and interesting, but whose emotional or instinctual life is immature. Another person has a capacity for deep feeling but is unable to find expression for it. No matter what the imbalance, it inevitably leads to feelings of frustration and dissatisfaction since part of that person's self is always lying dormant or battling against the rest of him instead of being freely expressed. Yoga works, through the body, to restore the balance, and removing energy blocks and chronic tensions is the way it goes about it.

PASSIVE AWARENESS OF DISCOMFORT

By eliminating bodily tensions through yoga practice, one gradually loosens the bonds of the ego so that one's awareness and full experience of life – the capacity for work and play – expands enormously. You move into one of the postures slowly and calmly and you find yourself in a state of stillness. Your senses are sharpened to what is happening inside and out. It is a kind of passive concentration that is almost without thought or imagery. As you move slowly through the posture, the feeling in your stiff body becomes more intense. It can sometimes be very painful. One's natural inclination is to get away from the discomfort by coming out of the posture, but the effectiveness of yoga depends on not allowing yourself to do this. Instead of either withdrawing from the asana or struggling hard to maintain it (the ways one would usually deal with discomfort) you simply allow yourself to go with the pain, to be in it until, surprisingly, it disappears. If you can do this, if you can keep your concentration on the posture itself, accepting the discomfort, then after it is finished you will feel exceptionally clear-headed, whole, and well-balanced.

But it takes a little discipline at first. Then after you've practiced yoga for a few weeks you realize you are feeling better all the time. And the effort of getting up that fifteen minutes earlier to go through a few new postures is no longer a chore but something you look forward to. You will also find that you are thinking in new ways and that lots of the energy which was once wasted in various internal conflicts is becoming available for you to use as you wish.

UNDERSTANDING ASANAS

Every woman has two kinds of energy, male and female. Male energy is like the sun – invigorating, stimulating, creative, and powerful. The male postures in yoga call forth this dynamic energy and release it.

Female energy is recuperative, calming, nurturing and gentle. The female postures are restoring to body, mind, and spirit. Yoga attempts to release male and female energies and ultimately to fuse them in union – to integrate the person.

The first four postures are male. They are done standing and they revitalize you. The last four are female and calming. In order to achieve the best balance and effect it is best to do them in the order recommended.

Do each posture slowly and deliberately, taking note of how your body feels with every movement.

BASIC YOGA

Never hold a position if you feel real strain, but do expect to feel some initial discomfort as your body stretches and loosens. The dicomfort will pass.

REVITALIZING STRETCHER

Stand with your hands at your sides, palms open, feet together so you are well balanced. As you inhale slowly, raise your arms above your head until your palms come together. Exhale, keeping the arm position and rise up on your toes. Now inhale again; be aware of the stretch in your spine. Hold your breath for a few seconds. Now exhale slowly, bringing your arms down to the starting position and coming down from your toes. Repeat this three times.

SHAKEDOWN

Standing with your feet a comfortable distance apart, start the exercise by shaking your hands loosely, but vigorously from the wrists, then work up the arms and shoulders, until you are shaking your your whole body vigorously. Then lift up one leg at a time and shake it too. The idea is to shake throughout the whole musculacture of the body and get rid of excess tension.

THIGH STRETCHER

Standing with your hands on your hips, your heels together and toes apart in a 'V' shape, slowly inhale, coming all the way down to a squatting position and keeping your back straight. Inhale and come up very slowly, pushing down on the balls of your feet. (It helps to keep your eyes fixed on something steady to balance.) With feet flat on the floor, exhale again, resting in the standing position. Repeat three times.

WINDMILL

Stand with your feet about three feet apart, arms hanging loosely at your sides. Inhale, raising your arms to clasp your hands above your head. Exhale, bringing arms down, with hands still clasped, in a circle to one side and then right down towards the floor. Go around three times in each direction.

KNEE TOUCHES

Lying on your back, inhale bringing one knee up to your chest. Exhale and bring your forehead up to meet your knee. Return to the starting position without inhaling again until you raise the other knee to repeat the movement. Repeat the exercise with each knee three times.

DOUBLE CONTRACTIONS

Do the preceding exercise with the same breathing pattern as before, but pulling both knees up at once and lifting your head to meet them with your forehead. Finish by rocking back and forth on your back. Repeat six times.

TUMMY TWISTS

Lying flat on your back on the floor with your arms spread wide to each side from the shoulder, inhale, bringing knees up, feet flat on the floor. Keeping knees together, exhale, knees twisting to the right and lowering to the floor, keeping shoulders flat and head straight. Hold for ten seconds, breathing normally through the nose. Then inhale, bringing knees up again slowly, and exhale, this time lowering them to the left. Repeat twice, alternating from side to side.

THE CORPSE

This is an excellent pose with which to begin and end a yoga session (see page 54). Use it to become fully aware of complete relaxation. You can rest in this pose after each asana, unless it is more natural to relax on your stomach, as with the Cobra, Locust and Bow.

Lying on your back with your arms at the sides of your body, palms facing upward, let your feet fall

THE CORPSE (CONTINUED)

open and your body go completely limp. Close your eyes. Take four deep breaths through your nose. Starting with your feet, concentrate on each part of your body right up to your face, allowing all the muscles to relax and your weight to sink into the floor.

EASY POSE

This pose is the basis for the neck and shoulder exercises, the eye exercises and the Lion pose. It is a classic position for meditation.

Sit cross-legged on the floor with your spine straight and your head erect. Rest your hands palms downwards on your knees. Allow your knees to drop downwards to the floor.

THE LION

This pose strengthens and improves circulation to the tongue, jaw and throat.
1. Sitting in the easy pose, inhale deeply through the nostrils, push your palms down on your knees and splay out your fingers.
2. Now breathe out vigorously, making an 'ahh' sound, opening your eyes as wide as possible and sticking your tongue out and down as far as it will go.
3. Hold the pose as long as you can, then retract your tongue, breathe in through the nose and let spine and hands relax.

Easy Pose

The Corpse

The Lion

HEAD ROLLS

This movement gently stretches the neck, toning the muscles and relaxing you at the same time.
1. Sit in the easy pose with the spine straight and the shoulders forward. Let your head relax forward. Turn it to the right and let the weight of it carry the head round to its natural limit.
2. Roll your head round to the back, letting it relax there for a few seconds.
3. Continue rolling your head round to the left, letting the neck bend as far as it can.
4. Let your head fall down as it comes round so that your chin ends pointing in towards your chest.

SHOULDER LIFTS

To release the tension in your shoulders and increase flexibility, start off by sitting in the easy pose described on the facing page.
1. Facing forward with neck straight, raise your right shoulder as high as it will go, then let it drop. Repeat with the left shoulder. Do this five times.
2. Raise both shoulders together. Let them drop into a relaxed position. Repeat five times.

EYE EXERCISES

If you exercise your eye muscles you can guard against eye strain and improve your eyesight. These exercises are ideally suited to a work break.

1. Rotate your eyes slowly, looking at the extreme points of your vision while keeping your head quite still. Repeat in the opposite direction.
2. Criss-cross the circle of your vision, focusing for a second or two at the end of each movement. Look up, then down, left, then right.
3. To exercise depth of vision, hold your hand up at a comfortable distance from your face. Focus on it, then gradually let your gaze move back from it into the far distance – you can look through the wall if there is one in the way. Now let your eyes travel back until your sight fixes once more on your hand.
4. To finish these exercises and relax your eyes, warm your hands by breathing on them and cup your palms over your closed eyes for a few seconds.

LEG RAISES

These exercises strengthen the leg muscles and those of the lower back and abdomen. They will also tone up your muscles ready for the headstand, besides trimming your waist and thighs. Except for position three, your back should stay flat on the floor and your head and shoulders should be relaxed. Begin each position with your legs together and your arms at your sides, palms down on the floor.

SINGLE LEG RAISES

1. Breathe in, lifting your right leg as high as you can. Lower it gently to the ground as you breathe out. Repeat with the other leg. Repeat the sequence five times.
2. Breathe in, lift your right leg and grasp it with your hands. Pull it down towards you as far as you can, trying not to raise your head and body from the ground. Hold the leg as close as you can and breathe in and out a few times.
3. Lift your chin up to touch the front of your leg, breathing in deeply as you do so. Breathe out, letting your head, arms and leg return to the ground. Repeat with the other leg.

DOUBLE LEG RAISES

This is a difficult exercise if your stomach muscles aren't strong. Practise the single leg raises first. To help yourself with the double leg raises you can knit your fingers together across your stomach and press down as you lift your legs. Your legs may be bent at the knee when you first raise them. Keep your bottom and the small of your back flat on the floor.

1. Lying flat on the floor, breathe in, raising both legs as you do so. Try to keep your legs straight and don't arch your back.
2. Lower your legs gently to the ground, breathing out as you do so. Keep your back flat.

SHOULDERSTAND

The shoulderstand benefits the body in a similar way to the headstand. In addition it stimulates the thyroid, because the chin presses into the base of the throat. It encourages deep breathing because it constricts the top of the lungs.

1. Lie flat on the floor with legs together and your arms by your sides with hands palms down. Push down on your hands and raise your legs high above your head.

2. Breathing in, lift your hips up and push your legs back over your head at an angle of about 45 degrees to the floor.

3. Breathing out, bend your arms up at the elbows and support your body with your hands, fingers behind and thumbs towards your face. Push your back up straight and lift your legs towards the vertical.

4. Straighten your spine, moving your hands as far down towards your shoulders as you can, and bring your elbows closer together. Hold your legs upright with feet relaxed. Press your chin into your chest and breathe slowly and deeply.

5. When you have maintained this pose as long as you wish, lower your legs right over your head, put your arms flat on the floor with palms down, and very slowly roll your back down onto the floor, feeling each vertebra as you go. When your back is flat, lower your legs slowly, keeping them straight and breathing out as you do so.

THE PLOUGH

The plough is the completion of the shoulderstand. The compression of the abdomen massages the internal organs.

1. Lie flat on your back with your arms at your sides and your palms on the floor. Breathe in and raise your legs. Breathe out. Breathe in and lift up your hips.

2. Supporting your back with your hands, breathe out and bring your legs down straight over your head towards the floor. Hold the pose here, breathing deeply, until you can comfortably touch the floor with your feet.

3. If you can touch the floor, walk your feet back as far as possible. Stretch your arms out behind your back and clasp your hands together. Breathe slowly and deeply. Come out as in the shoulderstand.

THE BRIDGE

In the bridge, the legs come down from the shoulderstand in the opposite direction to the plough (see pp66-6) and the body forms a perfect arch froom head to toe.

1. Get into the shoulderstand, supporting your waist with your fingers behind you and thumbs towards your face. Bend one leg back down to the floor in front of you.

2. Bend the other leg down to join it, so that your body forms an arch, bent at the knees.

3. Walk your legs out until your knees are straight. Keep your feet flat on the floor, your elbows as close together as possible. Take a few deep breaths. Inhale and come out of the pose via the shoulderstand and roll out.

THE FISH

To balance the stretch of the shoulderstand, plough and bridge, move into the fish pose. It exercises the muscles of the chest, neck and back and expands the ribcage.

1. Lie flat on your back. With your arms straight, put your hands underneath your thighs, palms down. Move your elbows as close together as you can.

2. Press down on your elbows. Breathing in, arch the small of your back. Stretch your neck, point your chin out as far as possible and rest the top of your head on the floor. Breathe deeply.

3. To come out of the Fish, first lift your head gently and then lay it back down on the floor gently. Then release your arms.

FORWARD BEND

This pose is not as easy as it looks. It stretches the entire body from the heels to the top of the spine. It stimulates the nervous system and the internal organs and reduces fat.

1. Lie flat on your back, feet together, with your arms stretched above your head, palms touching. Come up into a sitting position. Stretch your arms so that you can feel your spine growing longer.

2. Pull in the stomach muscles. Now breathe out, bringing your torso down to your knees, pushing it forwards, not allowing the spine to curve.

3. When your body has lowered to meet your legs, clasp them with your hands. Hold onto your toes. As you get more supple, you will be able to lay your palms flat on the ground in front of your feet. Point your toes backwards towards your head.

4. Inhale and come back out of the pose, still keeping your spine straight. Repeat three times, then hold the pose, breathing deeply.

THE COBRA

This pose massages the internal abdominal organs and is good for relieving period pains and constipation.

1. Lie down on your front with your palms flat on the floor under your shoulders and your forehead touching the floor.

2. Breathing in, push down with your hands and raise the body, stretching back with your head and curving your spine.

3. Let your body sink back to the floor again. Repeat this action two or three times, each time curving your spine a little further.

4. With practice you will be able to achieve the asana. Walk your hands backwards towards your body, curving the spine right back. Part your legs and bring your feet right up to touch your head.

THE LOCUST

The Locust complements the Cobra, strengthening the muscles of the legs, abdomen and lower back. Until your back gets more supple, you may be able to lift your legs only a few inches off the ground. In time, you will be able to bring them right over and touch your head with your feet.

1. Lie flat on your front. Breathe in and roll onto your side. Clasp your hands together in front of your thighs. Arms should be straight, elbows close together.

2. Breathe out and roll over onto your front with your arms beneath you. With your chin on the floor, take a few normal breaths.

3. Breathing in, push down on your hands and raise one leg, keeping it straight. Keep your leg in line with your body – don't stick it out to the side. Hold the position for two breaths, then repeat with the other leg. This is the Half Locust.

4. For the Full Locust, take a few deep breaths. Inhale, hold your breath and push both legs up at once. Hold the pose. Bring your legs down slowly. When you can get your legs right up, bend your knees and bring your feet down to your head.

THE BOW

The Bow tones the muscles of the spine. Rocking in the Bow position gives the internal organs a vigorous massage.

1. Lie down on your front with your forehead on the ground. Breathe in and bend your knees up, heels to buttocks. Catch hold of your ankles. Breathe out.
2. Breathing in, pull on your legs, raising thighs and chest from the floor. Look up. As your flexibility increases, try to keep your legs together.
3. Breathe out and rock forward, keeping your head up and back. Breathe in as you rock backwards. Relax and rest after this exercise.

THE HALF SPINAL TWIST

Most of the positions in this section stretch the spine backwards or forwards. As its name implies, this one gives flexibility from side to side. Keep your spine erect and your shoulders level.

1. Kneel down, legs together, sitting on your heels.
2. Sit to the right of your feet.
3. Lift your left leg and put it over and round the right. Rest your left ankle against your right leg. Keep your right foot tucked up against your bottom.
4. Keeping your back erect, stretch your arms out straight to the sides.
5. Twist your body to the left. Put your right arm down the outside of your left leg, so that the knee crosses under the armpit. Clasp your left foot with your right hand. Place your left hand palm down on the floor behind you and turn your body to the left, breathing out as you do so. Each time you do this, you should be able to twist a little further. Repeat, twisting in the opposite direction.

THE LOTUS

This is the classic pose for meditation. An erect spine and an effortlessly balanced body clears the mind and slows the metabolism.

1. Practise the Lotus by sitting with spine erect and the soles of your feet together. Press your knees down and forwards.

2. Sit with your spine erect, legs splayed out in front of you. Draw one foot in to the body and put it on the opposite thigh as close to your torso as you can.

3. Draw in the other foot. Tuck it under the opposite thigh for the Half Lotus. When your legs are more supple, put the second foot over the first on top of the opposite thigh and close to the body. This is the Full Lotus.

THE CROW

This is much easier to achieve than it looks. Keep your concentration on the act of balancing. The Crow strengthens the wrists, arms and shoulders.

1. Squat on your haunches with your arms inside your knees and your palms flat on the ground in line with your shoulders. Spread out your fingers so that they can take your weight.

2. Breathe in, concentrate on a point in front of you. Lean in towards it moving your weight onto your hands. Lift your feet up towards your bottom.

HANDS TO FEET POSE

This pose stretches the spine and leg muscles and slims the waist.

1. Stand straight, feet together. Breathe out. Breathe in, lifting your arms above your head. Stretch them as far above you as you can, feeling the spine grow longer.

2. Breathe out and fold your body forward, keeping

your back straight and your arms held out straight in front of you.

3. Bring your chest as far down to your thighs as you can, keeping your legs straight. Clasp your toes with your fingers or walk your hands back behind your feet and put them palms down on the floor.

THE TRIANGLE

1. Stand with your feet well apart. Turn your left foot outwards and your right slightly inwards. Stretch your left arm straight out and your right straight up against the side of your head. Breathe in.

2. Breathe out, bending over to the left. Let your left hand travel down your left leg. Hold onto it as low as you can. Keep your right arm against the side of your head and look out and up at your right hand. Repeat in the opposite direction.

TOTAL RELAXATION

Spend ten minutes in this pose after each yoga session. Lie flat on your back with legs and arms spread, toes and palms out. In order to relax properly, first tense each part of your body in turn, then let it go. Tense your feet and legs, then your arms and hands, face, shoulders, chest and buttocks, letting each relax in turn. Then think yourself into total relaxation, relaxing each set of muscles from your toes upwards. Feel the relaxation wash right over you and let it submerge you completely.

THE HIGH RAW DIET

RAW FOODS

When it comes to containing stress, diet is an all-important factor. A high raw diet, in which 75% of your foods consist of fresh fruits and vegetables, is the best possible way to manage stress nutritionally. An all raw regime for two weeks, or even just for a few days, will literally do wonders to revitalize your whole being – not just physically, but mentally as well, mentally and physically. It will also begin the process of the elimination of stored wastes within your body, which contribute to early ageing, banish chronic fatigue, and leave you feeling lighter and more joyous than you do now.

I would never have believed this had I not tried it for myself for several weeks. At that point, I became a terrible bore, for whenever anyone told me I look rdaiant I would launch into a diatribe about the virtues of raw food. Some of my friends bore my enthusiasm with patience and long suffering; others became intrigued and decided (sometimes openly, with my help in designing their diet, sometimes surreptitiously, so that I wouldn't know until after the event) to try it. Without exception, every one of them reported exactly the same results that I had had, although in different words.

A detoxifying raw food regimen for two weeks is the first step on the road to lasting health and beauty. It is also the only way to find out for yourself how much greater your potential for good looks, energy and emotional enthusiasm is than you probably believe. Finally, it is an excellent introduction to a better way of eating for life, for it can lead you on to a new, less restricted way of eating that will help to keep you permanently fit and well. You can use a raw food regimen in another way too; every few months you can go back to it for a few days to revitalize yourself whenever you feel you need it, particularly at the change of seasons, the end of each winter and the beginning of the autumn. You can also spend beneficial weekends on this regime whenever you have overindulged. It will straighten you out faster than anything else I know. But there is only one way you can find out what raw food can do for you; try it.

People often feel that a high raw diet sound restrictive, but this is only because they have not explored the delightful possibilities of such a regime – particularly true in the spring and summer when the days are warmer and raw vegetables are available in a wide and interesting variety. You will find that a diet that does not include any alcohol, anything cooked, no meat, fish, poultry or heat-treated dairy produce is in fact refreshingly easy to prepare and to keep to and wonderfully healthy.

RAW VEGETABLE SALADS

Choose three or more of the following and mix them together: lettuce, chicory, watercress, chopped apple, white heart of cabbage, carrots, radishes, fennel, raw sliced mushrooms, red and green peppers, Italian red lettuce, romaine, endive, spring onions, cucumbers, celery, herbs.

YEAR-ROUND SALAD SUGGESTIONS

IN SPRING

Choose one of the following mixtures:
1. Oranges, almonds, hazelnuts, knob celery, white cabbage, raw peas, celery, and fresh mint.
2. Apples and raw beetroot.
3. Strawberries, pine nuts, watercress, and lettuce.
4. Avocados, watercress, tomatoes, shallots.
5. Oranges, nuts, finely chopped spinach, a dash of horseradish.

IN SUMMER

1. Red currants, raspberries, nuts, and finely grated carrots mixed with fresh peas and finely chopped lettuce.
2. Peaches, cherries, almonds, garnished with lettuce and finely chopped tomatoes and sprigs of mint.
3. Apples, nuts, peaches, kohlrabi, parsley and red lettuce finely chopped.
4. Lettuce, watercress, grated carrots, celery, and spring onions.
5. Avocado, grapefruit, watercress, surrounded by a wreath of radishes and garnished with sunflower seeds.
These are the times of year always traditionally associated with salads – all the suggestions I've given above make extremely attractive main courses.

IN AUTUMN

1. Pears, almonds, hazelnuts, chicory, beets, and apples.
2. Knob celery, apples, nuts, and spring onions garnished with finely chopped spinach.
3. Cucumber, dill, lettuce, chopped spring onions and tomatoes.
4. Grapes, nuts, grated raw turnip, and grated raw carrot
Autumn is a time of mellow fruitfulness and all these salads reflect this mood.

IN WINTER

1. Oranges, nuts, winter cabbage, carrots, and watercress.
2. Tangerines, almonds, celery, watercress, and chicory.
3. Apples, nuts, grapes, turnips, and lettuce.
4. Fennel, spinach, chicory, and chopped tomatoes on a bed of lettuce.
5. Celery, pears, nuts, and Jerusalem artichokes garnished with chopped parsley.

These are just five suggestions – try your own mixtures and variations.

YOGHURT AND EGG DRESSING

1 egg yolk
1½ cups non-fat yoghurt
3 tablespoons lemon juice or cider vinegar

Pinch cayenne pepper
Fresh or dried herbs
2 teaspoons honey

Put ingredients into the top of a double boiler and stir over hot water until the mixture thickens. Refrigerate to serve cold or use hot on hot potato salad or hot rice salad to complement the taste.

TOMATO DRESSING

3-5 tomatoes (depending on size)

2 tablespoons lemon juice
½ teaspoon basil

Put into blender and liquefy. Store in refrigerator.

ALMOND-DATE TOPPING

1 cup raisins or dates, soaked in water for several hours to

plump them up
½ cup blanched almonds

Put into blender and liquefy. Store in refrigerator until just before serving.

AVOCADO-TOMATO DRESSING

4 small tomatoes
1 avocado
2 tablespoons lemon juice

Dash of Tabasco
Crushed clove of garlic or dash of garlic powder

Mix in blender. Store in refrigerator.

YOGHURT SWEET DRESSING

1 cup non-fat yoghurt
1 large orange, peeled, with
 seeds removed

1 tablespoon lemon juice
4 pitted dates
Dash of cinnamon, if desired

Put into a blender and mix well. Store in refrigerator.

THOUSAND ISLAND DRESSING

1 hard boiled egg, chopped
5 teaspoons celery, finely
 chopped
3 tablespoons onion, finely

chopped
2 tablespoons black olives,
 chopped
1/2 cup non-fat yoghurt

Mix all ingredients and serve chilled.

NON-OIL VINAIGRETTE

3 tablespoons dried skimmed
 milk
1/2 teaspoon Dijon mustard
2 teaspoons honey

Dash of pepper
Pinch of basil
1 clove garlic, crushed
2 tablespoons vinegar

Mix ingredients, adding vinegar last. Beat well or blend until smooth. Chill and use the same day.

SWEET LHASSI

1/2 cup non-fat yoghurt
1/4 cup ice water
4 ice cubes
Dash of cinnamon

Dash of ground cloves
Dash of nutmeg
Dash of mace
1 tablespoon honey

Mix in blender.

GRAPE DELIGHT

Handful red or white grapes,
 seeded
1 tablespoon raw honey

Juice of 1/2 lemon or lime
1/2 cup of Perrier or seltzer
2 ice cubes

Mix in blender. The lemon or lime complements the taste of the grapes, while the Perrier adds sparkle.

oven, set at its lowest temperature, for 10 minutes. Then turn the oven off and leave the yoghurt in it until set. (If necessary, switch the oven on again after a couple of hours to maintain the temperature).

Never heat the yoghurt above lukewarm, or you will kill the lactobacillus and the yogurt will not set. The process usually takes about 4-6 hours for a large pot of yoghurt. Allow to cool and then refrigerate. Serve cold.

SUGARLESS JAM

For serving on whole-grain toast. Mix a selection of fruit such as strawberries, peaches, pears, apples, cherries, apricots, pineapples, blackberries, raspberries, red currants and black currants with orange juice and blend to a purée. Add a little cornstarch and, stirring constantly, heat until thickened. Add a dash of cinnamon, nutmeg, ginger or vanilla to taste. Store in refrigerator. Serve hot or cold.

BANANA TOPPING

Purée bananas with strawberries, blackberries, raspberries or loganberries. Add honey. Serve immediately at room temperature.

APPLE BUTTER

Skin and core 2 pounds of sweet apples. Put into a heavy-duty saucepan with a couple of tablespoons of water (just enough to prevent burning), the juice of a lemon, a cup of raisins, and a teaspoon of cinnamon. Cook slowly and long until the volume is only one third of what it was and the mixture thickens. Remove from the heat, put through the blender, and store in the refrigerator to spread on toast, pancakes and fresh fruit.

MOCK CREAM

1 banana
1 tablespoon powdered skimmed milk
1 egg yolk
4 drops vanilla extract

Mash banana, add other ingredients, and mix well. Serve cold on fruit salads.

MILK PUDDING

4 ounces long-grain brown rice or whole tapioca or whole-grain bread
Powdered skimmed milk (the quantity to make 1 quart when reconstituted)
2 eggs

3 cups water
4 tablespoons honey or blackstrap molasses
½ cup raisins
Freshly ground nutmeg

Serves 4

Wash and drain the grains. Mix milk, eggs and water and add the grains or bread. Sweeten with honey or blackstrap molasses. Add raisins. Sprinkle nutmeg over surface. Bake in moderate oven (350°F, 180°C) for 45 minutes.

WHOLEMEAL BREAD

1 ounce fresh yeast
2 tablespoons honey
Up to 1 quart lukewarm water

3 pounds stone-ground wholewheat flour

Mix yeast and honey in a small bowl with ½ cup of lukewarm water. Leave in a warm place for ten minutes or so to froth up. Pour the yeasty liquid into the flour and gradually add the rest of the water, until the right consistency is attained – dough should be firm and pliable. Mix well. Divide the dough into three 1-quart bread tins that have first been greased and warmed. Put the tins in a warm place, cover with a cloth, and let dough rise for about 20 minutes. Bake in a hot oven (450°F, 200°C) for 35 to 40 minutes.

BAKED EGG SOUFFLÉ (SAVOURY OR SWEET)

8 egg whites
8 egg yolks

Pepper
Parsley

Fillings (optional)

Beaten tuna fish (canned in water, not oil)
Chopped sprouted grains, green peppers and tomatoes
Seasonal berries and currants

Beat egg whites until they form peaks. Whisk pepper and parsley into yolks. Beat in any filling, if desired. Fold the whites into the yolks. Turn into a nonstick container and cook for 25 minutes in a 325°F (160°C) oven.

THE LIFESTYLE DIET FOR HEALTH

The foods you eat have a dramatic effect on the way you look and feel. Follow the nutritional guidelines in this section to help you in your relaxation programme.

VEGETABLES

Foods to choose

You must eat at least two salads a day made from all sorts of raw vegetables. You can have unrestricted amounts of vegetables at mealtimes and between meals. When cooking vegetables, it is best to either bake them (potatoes, sweet potatoes and yams, squash, carrots, onions) or to steam them. They must be served without butter and oil. You can always munch raw vegetables when you are hungry between meals (carrots, celery, radishes, cucumbers, watercress, green peppers), and you may have up to three glasses of fresh vegetable juice a day.

Foods to shun

None

DAIRY PRODUCTS

Foods to choose

You may have skimmed milk or non-fat buttermilk (up to half a pint daily); cheese made from skimmed milk, such as non-fat cottage cheese (up to four ounces a day); or homemade yoghurt made from skimmed milk (up to four ounces a day). If you eat both cheese and yoghurt in the same day, then don't have your meat, fish or poultry allowance for that day.

Foods to shun

Avoid all added fats, including butter, margarine, and oils. Trim all visible fat from meat and fish before cooking. Dress your salads with dressings containing no oil. Whole milk contains too much fat, as do ordinary cheeses – both soft like Camembert and hard like Cheddar – cream, and sour cream.

SUGAR

Foods to choose

Wipe sugar completely off your nutritional map. You may take one tablespoon of blackstrap molasses a day (rich in sulphur, vitamins, and other minerals), and you can use two tablespoons of honey a day for sweetening if desired. Recent studies have raised suspicions about the long-term use of artificial sweeteners, so don't try to replace the sugar you have been used to with saccharine or other artificial sugar substitutes. Your palate will soon adjust to the natural sweetness of fresh fruits and you will get over your sweet tooth.

Foods to shun

Sugar in any form. Also reject anything made with sugar, such as sweets, desserts, chocolate, jams, jellies, and convenience foods that contain hidden sugar. Don't eat any condiments that contain sugar.

FRUIT

Foods to choose

Eat at least one piece of citrus fruit a day. You may have up to six pieces of other fruit as well. Fresh fruits are far superior to canned ones. If you have to eat canned fruits, make sure that they have not been canned in syrup. You may have as many as two glasses of fresh fruit juices a day, and up to one ounce of dried fruits, such as raisins, apricots, peaches, pears, dates and figs per day in place of two or three pieces of fresh fruit.

Foods to shun

None

FISH, MEAT, POULTRY AND EGGS

Foods to choose

Eat no more than four ounces of meat, poultry or fish three times a week, or two eggs daily. (Try to eat four to six eggs a week as they are an excellent source of the sulphur amino acids, which are essential for beautiful skin, hair and nails). Cut out smoked foods and fatty meats. All fat must be trimmed from meat and fish before cooking.

Foods to shun

None

NUTS AND LEGUMES

Foods to choose

Two or three times a week eat legumes – all sorts of beans and peas (except soy beans). You are allowed two ounces of nuts a day – raw and usalted and preferably mixed – but no peanuts.

Foods to shun

GRAINS

Foods to choose

You should eat all whole grains, such as brown rice, wheat, rye, barley, corn, oats, buckwheat and millet. Eat two or more kinds of whole grains each day, such as breads, cereals, or whole grain pasta, or in casseroles. You may also have one tablespoon of fresh wheat germ

Foods to shun

Avoid white flour and white rice, and anything made from refined grains such as ordinary pasta and most packaged breakfast cereals (which contain sugar as well as refined flours). Avoid breads with added oils. When you make your own, make it without oil or fat.

if desired; if ever you experience constipation, you may add two tablespoons of unprocessed bran to your salads, cereals, and soups.

CONDIMENTS

Foods to choose

Use as many herbs and spices as you wish in cooking. Avoid all bottled condiments that contain sugar, oils or fats. Worcestershire sauce, Tabasco and prepared mustard can be used without restriction. Mayonnaise is out, as are gravies, sandwich spreads, and monosodium glutinate. Do not add extra salt to your foods.

Foods to shun

None

DRINKS

Foods to choose

You can drink up to three glasses of fresh vegetable juice and two glasses of fresh fruit juice a day. You can have unlimited fat-free clear vegetable or chicken broth, and up to four cups a day of herb teas – camomile, spearmint and rosehip – sweetened with some of your daily honey allowance if desired. You can take coffee substitutes made from roots and grains. You are allowed seven glasses of wine a week and unlimited mineral and fresh spring water.

Foods to shun

Coffee and tea.

SUPPLEMENTS – GET TO KNOW

Some of the best supplements you can take for maintaining sleek, shining hair, youthful skin, a well-shaped body, and the unmistakable energy that marks a beautiful woman no matter what her age are not pills at all but foods such as liver and blackstrap molasses that are packed full of nutritional value in beautifully balanced forms that make them easy to assimilate. They are special foods – not exactly 'wonder foods', but then not far off it either. Many of them are rich sources of the 'protectors' – such nutrients as the important antioxidants vitamins C and E, the B complex with all its important value to nerves, hair and skin, selenium to improve the action of vitamin E and perhaps preserve cellular youth, and the sulphur amino acids. Get to know each of the super foods and make them an everyday part of your lifestyle diet.

LIVE SPROUTS

Sprout grains and seeds are without equal anywhere as powerhouses of live food nourishment. You can grow them on your windowsill or even in a warm dark cupboard. They are an excellent source of protein, minerals, complex carbohydrates, vitamins, and small quantities of essential fatty acids. Germinating seeds and grains increases enormously their nutritional value. Sprouted wheat, for instance, contains 30 percent more vitamin B than ordinary wheat grains, 200 percent more B2, 90 percent more niacin, and 80 percent more pantothenic acid. The vitamin C content increases 60 percent during sprouting. Similar increases occur in the germination of all the other sprouts too – alfalfa, aduki, mung beans, lentils, fenugreek and beans. Nowhere will you find a food more potent and valuable for health and beauty than sprouts. Germinated soybeans are so very rich in vitamin C, for instance, that a mere two tablespoons will supply you with the minimum daily requirement of vitamin C. (But don't stop at two – eat more!)

Sprouts are delicious on salads and in yoghurt and they are easy to grow in jars. The seeds themselves can be purchased from health food stores and ordered from sed suppliers. They can be sprouted literally anywhere during summer or winter, with or without light. So potent are they that if you lived on a mixture of sprouted greens alone you would have everything you need for health and long-lasting beauty.

THE SUPER FOODS

HERE'S HOW TO SPROUT

Put a heaped tablespoonful of seeds or grains into a jar, cover it with lukewarm water, and leave it overnight. In the morning, covering the jar with a piece of muslin or cheesecloth held in place with a rubber band, pour off the water and rinse the seeds in fresh lukewarm water (never hot or you will kill them). Now pour off the excess water through the cloth and put the jar on a windowsill. In the evening rinse again and pour of excess. Repeat the rinsing twice a day, and in three to six days (depending on the kind of seeds you have used) you will have sprouts to sprinkle on your salads, fill omelettes, or just eat as a snack. Grow a different kind in each jar and you will have a larder of nutritional delight.

EGGS

Eggs have been much maligned in recent years because of their cholesterol content, which was assumed to raise cholesterol in the blood and therefore was thought to contribute to coronary heart disease. Thinking on the subject is changing, for the egg is a balanced combination of nutritional goodness. It offers not only cholesterol (something your body makes anyway) but also zinc, sulphur, iron, phosphorous, unsaturated fatty acids and lecithin, all of which can enable your body to build its cholesterol into valuable steroid hormones.

Eggs are also the richest source of choline known, and they contain good quantities of biotin and also vitamins A, B2, D and E. Finally, they are a good source of the sulphur amino acids cystine and methionine, which appear to be important protective substances in warding off the ageing process. Try to eat four to six eggs a week, but never eat raw egg white.

BLACKSTRAP MOLASSES

A tablespoonful of blackstrap molasses supplies as much calcium as a glass of milk, as much iron as nine eggs, more potassium than any other food, and the B-complex vitamins in good balance. It is an extraordinarily valuable food for women who tend to be anaemic. The by-product of sugar refining, blackstrap molasses contains all the minerals, vitamins and trace elements lost in the refining process that makes sugar such an empty food. Blackstrap molasses is also rich in magnesium, vitamin E and copper. It is a great natural sweetener for yoghurt, muesli or drinks. A lot of skin troubles and hair problems respond to supplementing your diet with just a tablespoon of molasses a day. The taste varies greatly from one brand to another, so try them all until you find one that suits you. A cup of hot water into which you have squeezed the juice of half a lemon and added a tablespoon of molasses is an excellent way to start the day or a great pickup.

GARLIC

A powerful detoxicant, garlic, like onions, helps to clear fat accumulations from the blood vessels, lower cholesterol and protect against bacterial and viral infections. This evil-smelling little bulb has been used throughout history for a variety of medicinal purposes. Recently research has established that many folk uses of garlic are much more than old wives' tales. Garlic plays two important roles in the prevention of ageing. The first is to clear out wastes from the system, and to render harmless toxic substances that can cause heavy cell damage. (Garlic can even help clear dangerous heavy metals from the body). The second is to lower serum cholesterol and therefore help protect against arteriosclerosis, one of the worst manifestations of ageing.

KELP (SEAWEED)

Sea plants grow in mineral-rich seawater, which means that they contain a beautifully balanced combination of all minerals essential for life and health in any easily assimilable form. Kelp, or seaweed, is a superb source of iodine, which helps protect the body against radioactivity in the atmosphere that contributes to early ageing. It also strengthens hair and nails. Kelp is also rich in B-complex vitamins, vitamins D, E and K, as well as magnesium and calcium. You can use it dried in soups, fresh in salads, or in the form of kelp tablets to supplement your diet.

WHEAT GERM

The heart of the wheat kernel, wheat germ is the richest known source of vitamin E. It is also rich in magnesium, copper, manganese, calcium and phosphorous. And it is a superb source of protein to sprinkle on muesli or yoghurt. But be sure to keep it refrigerated in a tightly closed container and if possible buy it in vacuum-packed tins, because the oil in it oxidizes rapidly and it can go rancid. And don't eat too much, for wheat germ is rich in fat.

LECITHIN

High in phosphorous, lecithin joins with iodine, iron and calcium in the body to give energy to the brain, and helps in the digestion and absorption of fat, apparently breaking up cholesterol so that it can pass through artery walls. It has also been shown to increase immunity to virus infections and help prevent gallstones. This natural constituent of every cell of the body is available in some foods such as egg yolk, soybeans and corn. Supplementary lecithin comes in capsule, liquid and granule forms. It is a good source of essential fatty acids and choline. Lecithin has some rather remarkable benefits for health and beauty when taken daily – sprinkled into yoghurt or on a salad or simply taken from a spoon. It encourages the distribution of body weight and helps to cleanse the liver and purify the kidneys. As a result, and also because of its choline and unsaturated fatty acid content, it is wonderful for the skin. Lecithin is important in maintaining a healthy nervous system and vital to the resistance of stress-caused damage in the body.

LIVER

A powerhouse of anti-stress vitamins and protein, liver also contains good amounts of trace elements and minerals such as potassium, sodium and magnesium. It is a good source of phosphorous and sulphur amino acids – free radical scavengers thought to help protect against radiation. They may also play a part in the repair of damaged cells. The B-complex content of liver recommends it to any woman suffering from fatigue, working under stress or suffering from an illness. It can also improve on the health of your hair. When these B-complex vitamins are undersupplied, emotional and physical troubles can develop as well as some of the most annoying beauty problems – falling hair, prematurely greying hair and poor nails. Liver is also one of the richest sources of vitamin A, which is used with zinc and the B vitamins in the treatment of acne.

YOGHURT

A fermented milk product that is a mixture of lactobacillus acidophilus and other bacteria that keep the human intestine clean. The bacteria in yoghurt are antagonistic to the putrefying bacteria that can cause toxicity in the body. This is one of the reasons yoghurt is often useful in the treatment of skin disorders. It provides the B-complex vitamins, and it is richer in vitamins A and D than the milk from which it comes. Eating yoghurt daily – as well as raw vegetables in salads or whole-grain foods – prevents hidden constipation, which is so detrimental not only to health but to beauty. It is a source of protein that is alkaline-forming in the body, so it is excellent for avoiding hyperacidity. It is best to make your own yoghurt with powdered skimmed milk, for the yoghurt you can buy commercially often has had preservatives and flavourings added to it that interfere with its benefits.

BREWER'S YEAST

One of the best sources of B vitamins you can find, brewer's yeast contains seventeen vitamins, fourteen minerals and sixteen amino acids. An excellent source of enzyme-producing agents, it is a non-levening powder that you can add to juice, soups and breads. It has a slightly bitter taste (some brands are more bitter than others), but you get used to this if you start off with only small quantities of the stuff stirred into a glass of juice (tomato and pineapple mix with it particularly well) and then gradually increase the amount. You can also get brewer's yeast in tablets but in this form it is much more expensive and you have to take quite a few tablets to get even a teaspooon of it. Although there are other foods that are higher in chromium, the chromium is more nutritionally available to your body in brewer's yeast than in any other food. Chromium is essential for the maintenance of good blood sugar levels. There is also evidence that brewer's yeast may contain a factor vital to the body's immune response and, therefore, to your ability to resist infections and diseases; also, brewer's yeast and wheat germ taken daily may aid the prevention of heart trouble. Because the ratio between calcium and phosphorous in brewer's yeast is high on the side of phosphorous, you should mix the yeast with non-fat skimmed milk.

MIXED THREE SEEDS

Pumpkin, sesame and sunflower seeds ground in a blender or coffee grinder in equal proportions make a wonderful complete protein to sprinkle on yoghurt, salads or fruits. They are exceptionally rich in vitamins and have other qualities that make them excellent for hair and skin as well as overall health. They are all available in health food stores. You can grind a good quantity and then store them in the refrigerator. Pumpkin seeds are rich in B vitamins, phosphorus, iron and zinc. They are known to have a strong antiparasitic ability, and some European nature-cure specialists believe that they contain plant hormones which directly improve the hormonal functions of human sex glands. Sesame seeds, which the Romans first used along with honey as emergency supplies for their soldiers, are rich in magnesium and potassium and have been used for generations to treat chronic fatigue, insomnia and sexual dysfunctions. They are also very rich in calcium. In fact, they contain more calcium than either milk, cheese or nuts. They are also a good source of vitamin E, containing an amazing 31 milligrams of the vitamin in each 3½ ounce serving. They have twice the iron of raisins, three times as much as cooked eggs. This makes them particularly useful for women. They are also rich in the B-complex vitamins and are especially high in magnesium and zinc. The pectin in sunflower seeds is said to help eliminate radioactive strontium. Mixed together, the three seeds are a wonderful source of the essential fatty acids, which are vital for full bodily health. As well as treating the seeds as a source of wonderful sprinkles, as suggested above, use them as a substitute for sweets between meals.

THE QUESTION OF AGEING

Sleek, shining hair, youthful skin, a well-shaped body and the unmistakable energy that marks a beautiful woman no matter what her age are not accidents of nature. They depend on care. They also depend on protection. For ageing is no longer considered an inevitable consequence of the passage of time. How quickly and how badly you age depends not only on your genetic makeup, but also on how you live and what kind of attack you are exposed to in terms of stress, environmental pollution and wrong nutrition, all of which bring about ageing on a cellular level.

The ageing process itself is not completely understood. But scientists are in agreement that the foundation of the ageing process lies in the individual cells themselves, which in turn make up the tissues, organs and systems of the body. At cell level two important things happen as you age. First, there is a disruption of the DNA and RNA – the systems in your cells which are responsible for preserving and reconstructing genetic information for growth, synthesis of new proteins and reproduction. Second, there is a progressive tendency for more cells to die than your body is able to replace.

Radiation is one cause of these things (and one of the reasons lying in the sun causes the skin to age rapidly). The genetic material, the DNA with its chromosomes, needs to remain intact in order for cells to reproduce themselves accurately. Radiant energy penetrating the cell membrane can result in the formation of 'free radicals'. These are highly reactive molecular groups that combine with the DNA enzymes or cell membranes and cause damage, particularly in the chromosomes so that the whole genetic record of the cell becomes distorted.

But free radicals are not only the result of radiant energy, they are also produced by the interaction of oxygen with polyunsaturated fats, which results in formation of semistable peroxides that are in turn destructive to body proteins. When chromosomes are damaged either by free radicals or chemical reactions, some of the genetic information carried by the DNA is lost so that either the life of the cell itself is endangered or vital cell functions are impaired. This in turn leads to a further mis-synthesis of protein in the making of new cells and creates 'clinkers' that interfere with the normal immunological reactions and use up important nutrients needed for other things in the body, as well as strangling the life in cells with waste material.

The whole process is not yet completely understood, but what is known is that protection from radiation and from other factors which bring about alterations in the genetic material is an important part of any programme for preserving youth and beauty. Experimentally, one of the most successful ways to slow down the ageing process has been to destroy the free radicals before they can produce their multiplicity of harmful reactions.

Another phenomenon in ageing is the formation of 'cross-linkage' of molecules, where neighbouring molecules are chemically joined by a bridge or bond between an atom of one and an atom of the other. Well-known age researcher Johan Bjorksten has studied the cross-linkage phenomenon and pointed out that 'many of these cross-linked molecules lead to agglomerates which cannot be broken down by any body enzyme, but will increase in the cell and gradually crowd out other constituents, thereby causing a continual decline in the cell's activity and ability to cope with stress'.

Certainly cross-linking is an important phenomenon in the ageing of the skin. Collagen, a protein that makes up 30 percent of the body's total protein content and is largely responsible for giving young skin its resilience and the muscles their firmness, is particularly vulnerable to cross-linking and its various undesirable effects.

When collagen fibres start to cross-link and to bind together, wrinkles form and the body loses its firm curves and perfect shape. Whatever can be done to neutralize the effects of free radicals and thereby protect the genetic material of cells, or to inhibit the process of cross-linking, will also help to preserve skin and body shape and hold back the rate of ageing and the dramatic effects on your body and state of mind that these can bring.

How does all this relate to stress and relaxation? The answer is simple. Stress is not simply a mental state, or indeed a response to mental or outside pressures. It has physical causes as well. So, if your body itself is not in sufficient shape to meet the challenges it faces, you may well become stressed as a result, or lose the ability to relax as easily as you should. Learning how to come to terms with, understand and control stress involves the whole you; if you look your best, you will also feel it and so be able to cope all the better with life's stresses and strains. In addition, how well or badly you cope with stress is directly linked to ageing rates.

MASSAGE

WHY MASSAGE?

The sense of touch is the new-born baby's primary contact with the world. Babies and all young animals snuggle up to their mothers for reassurance, warmth, comfort and security, and as they grow, touch – rough and tumble and tickling – becomes an important part of their play.

Physical contact with other creatures has long-term effects on development as well as short-term benefits. Experiments carried out on rats and mice showed that creatures isolated from each other and denied touch grew much more slowly than others kept in similar conditions that were frequently stroked and cuddled. The ones that were stroked and cuddled were stronger, sturdier, more active, less prone to infection and less timid than those in solitary confinement.

This would have come as no surprise to the American psychologist S.M. Jourard, who showed over twenty years ago that adult humans who are frequently touched tend to have more confidence and more self-esteem than those who are deprived of affection.

Yet often adults will go out of their way to avoid touching each other. A handshake in greeting, a slap on the back between men, or a peck on the cheek between women is all we allow ourselves. Touch is taboo – we jump a mile when we touch each other by accident, because we are brought up to believe that touching is something you do only in bed.

Massage is a way of bringing touch back into your life and using it to soothe, to calm, to relieve tension and to transmit caring. It is a wordless communication of affection and understanding that can be given by any one human being to another – no particular skills are required, though the techniques described on the following pages are useful.

Massage is distinct from erotic massage because it relaxes, rather than excites, though, of course, it can be used as a prelude to exotic massage. It releases the tension from aching muscles, stimulates blood flow and eases stress, as the receiver's tangled thoughts give way to a simple sense of wholeness and peace.

BEFORE YOU START

Massage is a healing art and needs to be carried out in harmonious and comfortable surroundings so that both giver and receiver can achieve the ideal kind of floating concentration on what is happening. The giver ought to be relaxed from the start, as otherwise tensions could be transmitted to the recipient.

A QUIET ROOM

The room in which you give a massage should be warm, draught-free and softly lit. Draw the curtains and take the phone off the hook to avoid distractions, and choose a time when no-one else is in the house. Unless you have a person-sized table that you can cover with blankets, your friend will be most comfortable lying on pillows or a mattress on the floor.

CLOTHING

It is best to receive a massage in the nude, as skin-to-skin contact is what it's all about, but wear the minimum of clothing if it makes you feel more comfortable. The giver should be loosely dressed for free and easy movement.

OIL

One of the pleasures of massage can be the use of a specially scented oil – you can add a few drops of concentrated oil of cloves, cinnamon or lemon according to mood, to an odourless vegetable oil such as safflower, or you can choose a more expensive and subtly scented oil, such as olive oil or almond oil. Baby oil gets absorbed into the skin too quickly – as do creams and lotions – to be of much use.

Some of the strokes illustrated on the following pages can work without oil, but most of them work better with it, as it allows the hands to follow more smoothly the lines of the receiver's body. Talcum powder can be used if you have no oil, but it is not really a satisfactory alternative.

Your oil will need to be in a – preferably spill-proof – plastic bottle, as you will be moving round all the time and are bound to knock over a bowl or saucer, with disastrous results to the session, not to mention the mess on the carpet. A bottle at either end of the receiver's body is ideal, so that one is always in reach.

Never apply oil directly onto your friend's body – it can be quite a shock. Lightly oil your hands, which should be clean and warm, with nails clipped short, before you touch your partner.

MAKING CONTACT

When you make contact with your friend's body you will transmit your feelings through your hands. So it's no good giving a massage if you're tense, unhappy or unwell. You should be relaxed and well disposed towards your partner. You should also be physically comfortable. Sit or kneel so that your body is well balanced and free from strain. Use the movement of your torso to apply pressure, not just your arms and hands.

Once you have begun the massage, never break contact with your friend's body – make sure you are still touching him or her with your wrist or forearm even when you are oiling your palms.

Finally, try to rid your mind of thought completely and concentrate on the healing power in your hands.

BASIC STROKES

Your contact with your friend's body should be both firm and gentle. Try not to make jerky or uncertain movements. Don't be afraid to use your body weight to exert pressure, at the same time being constantly aware of, and sensitive to, the contours of the body beneath your hands. The trick to acquire is an acute sense of awareness, so that you never exert too much pressure, but, at the same time, do not negate your efforts by using too little.

Feel free to vary both speed and pressure from area to area, but change smoothly from one rhythm and one pressure to the next. If you are at one with your hands, they will lead you instinctively into the next phase of the massage when the time for such a change is right.

Your aim is to treat each part of your friend's body so that he or she is aware of each bone, each muscle, and then to intergrate this awareness into a sense of wholeness. Like any art, this takes time to perfect, but there is no real reason why it should be beyong anyone's grasp, unless, of course, your mental attitude is wrong and you yourself are tense and irritable. In such a case, switch roles and get someone to give you a massage!

There are four kinds of basic strokes.

Gliding strokes smooth gently over the skin, not penetrating deeply into the muscles.
1. Use long strokes, for example up your friend's back and down his sides to spread the oil, and as an introduction to more specific treatment.
2. Use light feathery strokes, touching your friend's skin

with the fingertips of first one hand and then the other, as a gradual lead-up to a break in contact.

Medium-depth strokes stretch and tone the softer areas of the body, relax muscle tension and aid circulation. The hands are used alternately to knead, pull and wring the flesh. The movements are sure and rhythmic.
1. In kneading, grasp and squeeze the flesh from one hand to the other, as if you were working on dough. Maintain a rocking movement.
2. From your position on one side of your friend's body, pull the flesh on his other side towards you, dragging your hands from the table or floor up towards his back. Work with alternate hands all down his side.
3. Put one hand on the far side of your friend's body, the other on the near side. Pull your far hand towards you and simultaneously push your near hand away. Reverse the direction and move continuously along the body, repeating this wringing action.

Deep tissue strokes are specific and penetrating. You use your fingertips, your thumbs and the heels of your hand, gradually working deeper to rid the body of inner tension. Your hands should be strong and relaxed, with your body weight behind them.
1. Making tiny circular motions with your fingertips, feel your way down into the joints and work gradually and thoroughly around them.
2. Working on a small area at first, push your thumbs alternately over it, building up into larger circles or moving on to free the next muscle from tension.
3. Push the heels of your hands forward one after the other onto your partner's flesh, as if they were walking on the spot.

Percussion As the name implies, this is quite a vigorous approach, and not always a suitable part of a massage sequence. It stimulates the circulation and tones the skin.
1. Hacking. Your hands and wrists should be relaxed. Hold your hands out, palms facing and bounce them up and down alternately on your friend's body. Work on flesh areas until you have a good enough rhythm to work on the muscles.
2. For pummelling, work as in hacking, but with fists clenched. Keep your wrists relaxed, as if you were playing the bongo drums.
3. Now cup your hands and repeat the drumming motion. This is quite noisy because of the suction effect of your cupped palms on your partner's skin.
4. Pinch up small ripples of flesh between your fingertips. Work with alternate hands, letting the flesh subside as you release it.

THE BASIC MASSAGE

Once you get used to giving massage, you will be able to allow your hands to lead the way – in the meantime it's useful to follow certain guidelines. First gently oil the area to be massaged. Begin with light general strokes, working gradually more deeply and more specifically, then take your friend out of the massage with increasingly lighter strokes again.

You can begin with the back and travel down the legs, then ask your partner to turn over and work on the face, including the eyes (make sure he or she isn't wearing contact lenses), then down the neck to the shoulders, chest and abdomen. Massage each arm and leg, working up the limb with firmer strokes towards the heart, and down it more lightly to the toes and fingers. Finish with broad connecting strokes, or with your hands at rest on two parts of the body to give your friend a sense of completeness. Repeat all the movements as many times as you like.

THE BACK

More time is usually spent massaging the back than any other part of the body – not just because it's the largest area, but because back massage gives the greatest sense of release.

1 Long stroke Sit at your friend's head. Oil your hands and warm them by rubbing them together. Put your hands flat on the back at either side of the top of the spine (without touching it – this is not pleasant), fingers pointing in. Push your hands smoothly down the back, exploring its contours, travel round the buttocks and bring them up the sides to the starting position.

2 Buttocks Sit to the side of your partner's thighs to work on the lower back, a very high tension area, and the buttocks. Work from first one side, then the other, massaging the side of the body opposite you. Knead the buttocks, squeezing and wringing your way around them. Then pull up the sides of the hips, working your way up to the waist.

3 Lower back With circular kneading motion, but keeping your hands fairly flat, work broadly all over the lower back.

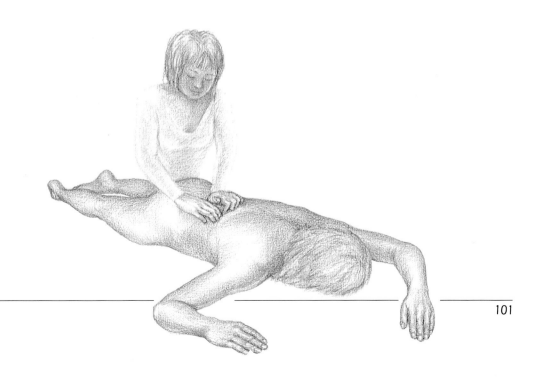

4 The spine In general, avoid touching the spine, except for a stroke called the 'rocking horse'. In this, you place your right hand on the base of your partner's spine, your left hand over it. Push your hand right up to the top of the spine, keeping the pressure steady. Come back down the spine with your middle and index fingertips tracing a line on either side of it and your second hand following close behind the fist.

Then work your thumbs up the spine, making little circles on either side of it. Loosen any tension knots as you work your way up and down.

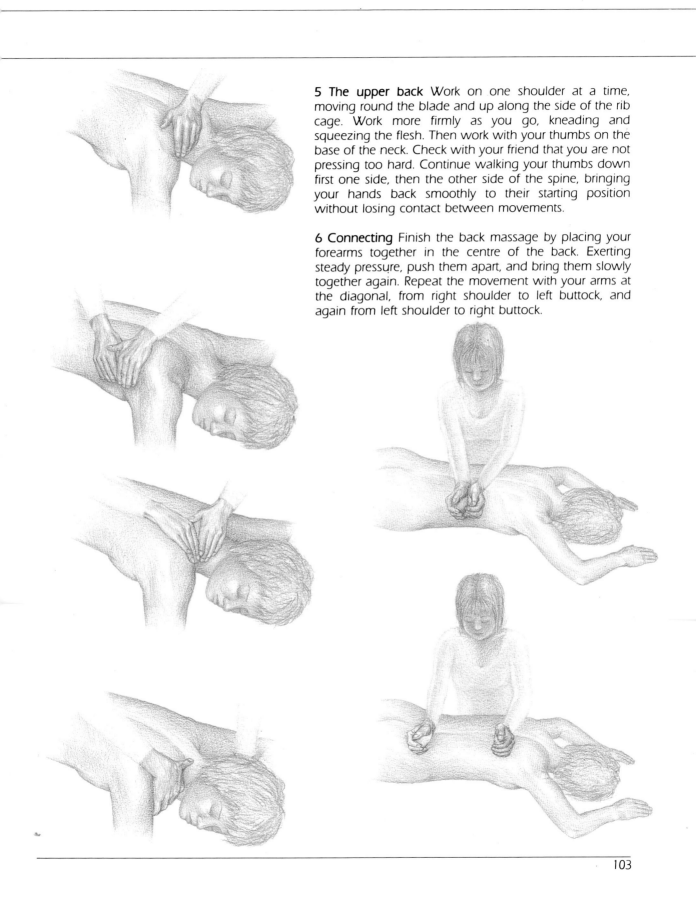

5 The upper back Work on one shoulder at a time, moving round the blade and up along the side of the rib cage. Work more firmly as you go, kneading and squeezing the flesh. Then work with your thumbs on the base of the neck. Check with your friend that you are not pressing too hard. Continue walking your thumbs down first one side, then the other side of the spine, bringing your hands back smoothly to their starting position without losing contact between movements.

6 Connecting Finish the back massage by placing your forearms together in the centre of the back. Exerting steady pressure, push them apart, and bring them slowly together again. Repeat the movement with your arms at the diagonal, from right shoulder to left buttock, and again from left shoulder to right buttock.

THE BACK OF THE LEGS

The sciatic nerve runs from the base of the spine down the back of the legs to the heel, so massaging the backs of the legs is very good for people suffering from pain or stiffness in the lower back.

1 Long stroke Sitting at the feet, cup both your hands over your friend's ankle, one in front of the other. Move your hands up the leg, let them part just below the buttocks and return to the ankle, one travelling along the inside of the thigh and the other along the outside.

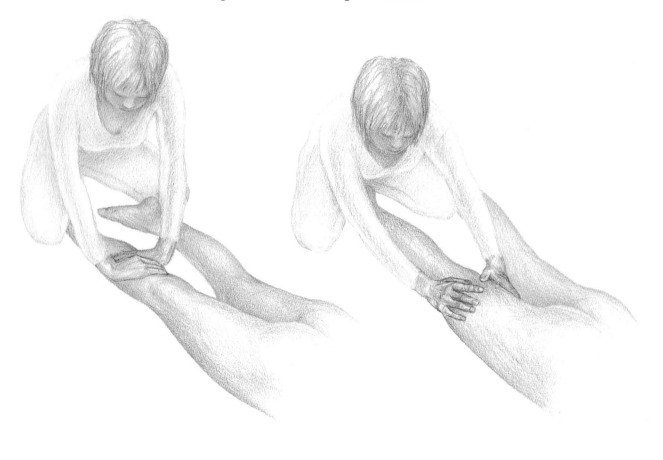

2 Draining the leg The purpose of these strokes is to stimulate the circulation by increasing the flow of blood back to the heart. Work up the legs from the ankles to just below the buttocks, then sweep back down.

Clasping your hands around the calf, walk up it with your thumbs, using short, firm strokes. Be gentle when you get to the knee to avoid pushing it uncomfortably onto the floor.

Work up the thigh, kneading with the heels of your hands. Work slowly and rhythmically, using broad, deep strokes.

3 Working down the leg Work back down the leg using kneading and wringing strokes. Maintain continuous contact, not lifting your hands up between movements. Finish by pulling the flesh on the inside of the thigh. Start just above the knee and work up and down again a couple of times.

THE FOOT

The foot is an extremely complex structure of twenty-six bones. It carries the entire weight of the body and is important from a psychological as well as a structural point of view as our connection with the ground. In addition it carries tens of thousands of nerve endings that connect with every single part of the body, and this is how zone therapy – healing through foot massage – came to be developed to treat the entire body. If you are short of time, it is better to give your friend a foot massage than to concentrate on any other area.

1. Work over the entire sole of the foot with both your thumbs, holding the foot with your fingers. Prop the heel on a pillow, or on your own leg if necessary. Be slow and thorough.

2. Now work on the top of the foot, pressing firmly all over it with your thumbs. As you come to the ankle bone, use your fingertips.

3. Work around the ankle with one hand, exploring the bones and supporting the foot in your other hand. When you get past the ankle, clasp the leg and rotate the ankle by moving the foot in a wide circle, first one way and then the other, to improve flexibility.

4. Now turn your attention to the toes. Hold the foot in one hand. With the other, get hold of each toe in turn and pull it, twisting gently from side to side until your fingers slide off the toe.

5. Finish the foot by holding it between your palms, one on top and the other below. Centre yourself and stay quite still for a moment, imagining your energy flowing into your friend's body.

Now get your friend to turn over so that you can work on the front of the body. Start at the top and work down.

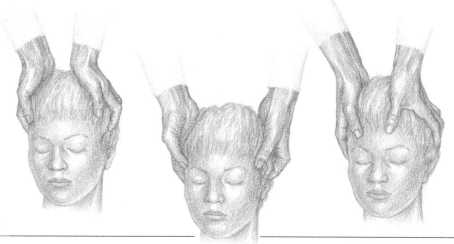

THE FACE

The face is so expressive of our emotions that we often try to hide what we feel beneath a mask of fixed expression. A face massage soothes away tension and allows the muscles to relax and the expression to be what it is – a reflection of the person within.

1. Begin with your thumbs together in the centre of the forehead near the hairline and move them out to the temples. Describe a circle with the balls of your thumbs and move back to the centre. Circle again. Continue this sequence, moving down the forehead to the eyebrows.

2. Press with your two forefingers into the eye sockets right at the top of the nose (having made sure that your friend is not wearing contact lenses) and draw the fingers out and over the brows.

3. Draw your fingers gently across the eyelids from the inside to the outside. Lift your fingers to return to the inside.

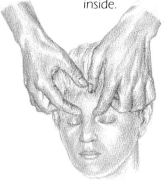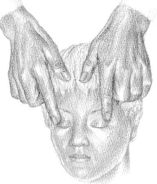

4. Draw your fingertips across the cheekbones, out towards the jaw and up towards the ear, working slowly and firmly.

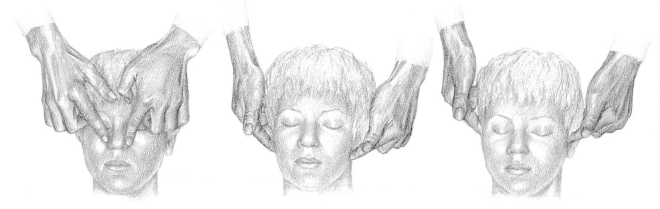

5. Stroke outwards from the centre above the top lip. Repeat beneath the bottom lip.

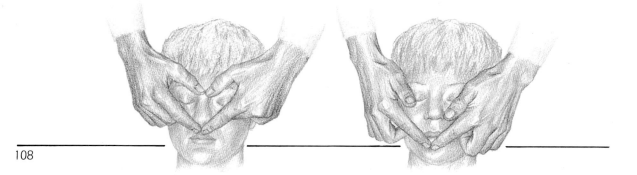

6. Work from the tip of the chin round the jawline, pulling the flesh gently between thumb and fingers.

7. With the heels of your hands touching above the nose and your fingers curling round the jawline, slide your hands gently over the cheeks and round the jaw up to the ears, pulling them out and up from the head.

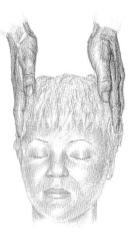

8. Finish by moving your hands in a long connecting stroke over the face, under the chin and up round the back of the neck. Begin with the heels of your hands on the forehead, palms cupping the eyes. Rest there for a moment, then move down over the cheeks, up round the jaw and out behind the ears.

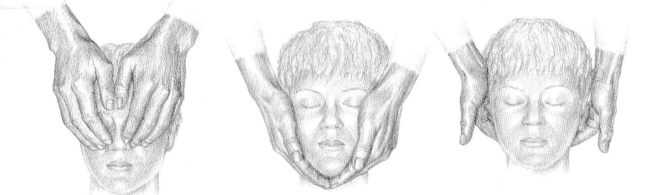

MASSAGE

FRONT OF TORSO

Study your friend's breathing before working on this part of the body, so that you move with, instead of against it. The soft belly is a vulnerable area, so treat it gently. If your partner is ticklish, avoid short fingertip strokes and concentrate on broad, firm strokes with the flat of the hand.

1 Long stroke To oil the torso, place your palms together on the upper chest, push them smoothly down the body to just below the navel, and bring them back up the sides.

2 Chest Work over the chest under the collarbone, pressing the fingertips in tiny circles and drawing your fingers outwards. Work down the whole rib cage in this way, following the lines of the bones. If your partner is a woman, avoid the fleshy part of the breasts and the ribs immediately beneath them, as this doesn't feel pleasant.

Pull up the sides of the body from the waist to the armpit. Knead the pectorals, then let your hands glide up the other side of the body.

3 Stomach Move to your partner's side, keeping body contact as you do so. Rest both your hands gently on the stomach and let them describe clockwise circles round the navel. The direction is important – it is the direction of the large intestine. Increase pressure as you go, describing smaller circles with your fingertips so that you are moving in spirals like a telephone cord around the navel. Time your movements to synchronize with your partner's breathing.

ARMS AND HANDS

The arms and hands are instruments of giving and receiving, defending and attacking. The muscles in the shoulders and hands get particularly tense with pent-up feelings of defense or aggression, and massage can release this tension.

1 Long stroke Clasp your oiled hands around your partner's wrist, thumbs together. Move the hands together up the arm, separating them at the top so that one hand goes up and over the shoulder, returning to the wrist on the outside of the arm, and the other travels back down the inside of the arm.

2 Draining the forearm The purpose of this movement is to stimulate the lymphatic flow and the return of the blood to the heart. Raise the forearm, holding the hand with one of yours. Circle the inner wrist with the fingers and thumb of your other hand and squeeze lightly, sliding your hand down to the elbow. Bring your hand back up without applying pressure and repeat.

3 Draining the upper arm Bend your friend's arm across his chest so that the elbow sticks up in a 'V' in line with his nose. Grasp the arm with both hands, thumbs together, and pull down firmly from the elbow to the shoulder. Slide the hands gently back up and repeat.

4 Stretching the arm Take hold of the wrist in one hand and place the arm above the head. Run your other hand down your partner's side and press in at the waist. Push with both hands so that his arm and side are stretched in one.

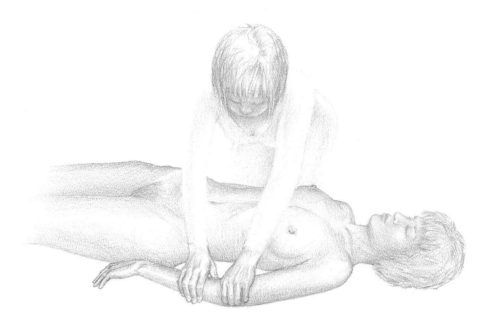

5 Kneading the arm Knead and wring all the way down the arm to the wrist, exploring the elbow joint en route.

6 The wrist Work in circles across the whole wrist, plucking the skin between thumb and forefinger.

7 The palm Open the palm as you would open a book, turning it outwards. Stretch the hand gently until it is flat and then massage as shown.

8 The back of the hand Hold the wrist in your left hand. With the fingers of your right, explore the grooves between the bones of the hand, working up to the fingers.

9 Fingers Move on to the fingers, pulling your fingers up them and twisting as you let go.

THE FRONT OF THE LEGS AND THE FEET

Ending a massage with the legs and feet helps your friend get back to earth

1 Long stroke Kneel astride your partner's foot and put your oiled hands together, cupping his ankle. Move them firmly up the leg, let them part at the top and return one hand over the hip and back down the outside of the leg, and the other back down the inside of the leg. Move your hands back gently, feathering with your fingertips if you wish.

2 Draining the lower leg Put your hands one in front of the other across the ankles, making a 'V' between your thumb and your index finger. Push them firmly up the shin to the knee and bring them back lightly down the sides of the calf.

3 The kneecap With your fingers behind the knee, overlap your thumbs above it. Move them in overlapping circles around the kneecap – a surprisingly pleasant sensation!

4 Draining the thigh If your partner has very long legs, you may need to move to his side. Put your hands side by side just above his knee, thumbs together and pointing upwards, fingers to the back of the leg. Push firmly up towards the groin, allowing your hands to part at the top of the leg and down again.

5 Working down the leg Knead, wring and pull handfuls of flesh down the thigh from the hip to the knee, working quite vigorously. Work precisely with the fingertips around the knee, then continue squeezing the flesh on either side of the shin bone down to the ankle. Avoid pressure on the shin bone as it can be painful.

6 The foot Finish by giving the foot a final stroke, to bring your partner back down to earth. Open the foot by spreading it from the top to the sides, squeezing with your hands and pressing down firmly with your thumbs. Finally clasp the foot between your palms, one above and the other below. Gradually draw your hands off over the toes.

CONNECTING

The final movement in massage is designed to restore all the individual parts of the body that have come to life separately under your hands to one whole being. There are two ways of doing this. You can use long connecting strokes that go either from head to toes and fingers, or you can simply let your hands rest on your friend's body in two separate places, such as forehead and belly.

When the massage is over, cover your friend with a soft rug and let him rest in peace for a few moments to regain his bearings.

SELF-MASSAGE

No-one knows your body as well as you do – no-one else understands just where the pain is, what feels good or bad or how much pressure you can bear. For these reasons you might think that you can be your own best masseur or masseuse, but it's not true.

An obvious disadvantage is that you can't reach all the parts of the body that you need to get at. A less obvious, but equally big disadvantage is that you can't relax and enjoy massage at the same time as concentrating on giving one. And then there's the question of energy. In massaging a friend, you are ridding his body of negative charges and fuelling it with your own positive ones. There is no recharging of energies when you massage yourself.

But anyone who's keen on giving massage will want to know what it feels like – and where better to start than on your own body? You can practise your technique and maybe get a bit of relief from aches and pains at the same time.

Specific directions are not really necessary – just squeeze and pull, press and poke as hard as is comfortable – and remember anything that feels good so that you can try it out on your friends!

SHIATSU

Shiatsu is a healing art from Japan. The name means 'finger pressure'. Pressure from thumbs, palms, elbows and knees as well as fingers is brought to bear on acupuncture points in the body to balance its functions and encourage good health and energy.

The acupuncture points, called tsubos in Japanese, are

located on the body's meridians, channels through which flows the life force, Ki. Each meridian is connected to a vital function of the body, and pressure at the tsubos along the meridian will improve that function, relieving anything from colds to migraine or period pains.

Shiatsu is not difficult to learn and can be incorporated into a normal massage. Giver and receiver should be comfortable, warm and relaxed, and wearing loose clothing (the illustrations here have been drawn without clothes, so that you can see clearly what you are trying to achieve). The giver's body should be well-balanced at all times, so that the pressure that is being applied can be controlled without tiring. Pressure should be firm, steady and come from the whole body, not just the hands.

1 The back Apply pressure down both sides of the spine between the vertabrae, first with your palms, then with your thumbs. Treatment of the back stimulates the spinal nerves, and these supply all the internal organs. The points at the top of the back relate to the lungs and heart, those on the middle back to the digestive system; the lumbar area is connected to the kidneys, and the sacrum to the bladder.

2 The hips Apply thumb pressure to the points on the sacrum to relieve pelvic congestion, including menstrual tension and cystitis. Squeeze the sides of the buttocks with the heels of your hands to soothe lower back pain, which is often caused by long-term repression of sexuality or anger.

3 Back of legs and feet Work on one leg at a time. Press all the way down the centre, first with your palms, then with your knees. Supporting the kneecap, use thumb pressure on the back of the knee to relieve sciatica. Press the ankle points to stimulate the kidneys.

4 Chest Open up the chest by pressing on the shoulders with the heels of your hands. Thumb pressure on the points indicated stimulates the lungs. Press in each groove between the ribs to relieve congestion in the chest.

5 Arms and hands Treatment of this part of the body stimulates elimination through the skin and lungs as well as the bowels. The 'great eliminator',the point between thumb and forefinger, rids the body of colds, headache and toothache. Apply thumb pressure for five seconds. The point at the centre of the palm exerts a calming influence over the mind and emotions, and the one at the end of the elbow crease relieves arm and shoulder pain.

6 The hara The hara, the Japanese word for the abdomen, is the seat of the Ki, the life force. Treatment of the hara is a healing art in itself, as it can be divided into zones that connect with the entire body. The points at either side of the navel can be pressed in towards it to stimulate the digestion and relieve stomach cramps. The tan-den, a hand's breadth below the navel, should be pressed deeply with the flat of your fingers to revitalize the whole body.

7 Front of legs and feet This area connects with the liver, the spleen and the stomach. Press all the way down each leg with your palm, then down the inside of the thigh, with your partner's leg crooked at the knee. Rotate the kneecap and press the point below the knee to stimulate energy and well-being. The point four fingers up from the ankle bone brings relief from period pains, the one on the inside of the heel stimulates the kidneys, and the one above the join of the big toe and second toe promotes the function of the liver.

REFLEXOLOGY

Reflexology is a very subtle art of healing that can be mastered only after years of practice. Its origins are probably as ancient as those of acupuncture and shiatsu.

Reflexology as it is today was defined this century by two American practitioners, Dr William H. Fitzgerald and Eunice Ingham. Dr Fitzgerald developed the idea of zone therapy. The theory is that the feet and hands can be divided into ten zones (one for each digit) that run right through the body. Thus, there are points on the feet and hands that correspond to every organ and function of the body, and malfunctions can be treated by pressure on these points. Eunice Ingham discovered that the reflexes in the feet were more responsive than those in the hands.

The main benefit you can confer on your partner as a amateur reflexologist lies not in the diagnosis and treatment of disease, which takes expert knowledge, but in relief from tension and improved circulation.

Reflexology can be carried out anywhere, any time. Sit your friend in an easy chair, legs propped up so that the feet are level with your hands as you sit in front of him.

REFLEXOLOGY AND RELAXATION

It takes a qualified practitioner to diagnose and treat disease by reflexology, but as a beginner you can certainly use the simple technique illustrated below to great advantage in helping your friend to relax.

1 Side to side Hold the foot between the palms of your hands with your thumbs upwards parallel to the big and little toe. Roll the foot from side to side, pushing with the heel of one hand and pulling with the fingers of the other, and then reversing the process. Do this quite rapidly, until the foot becomes flexible.

2 Diaphragm and solar plexus flexing The diaphragm and solar plexus run across the foot just below the ball. Grasp the toes of the right foot with your left hand and push them back, pressing your right thumb firmly on the inside edge of the reflex. Now pull the toes towards you against the pressure of the thumb. Continue across the foot to the outside edge of the reflex.

3 Ankle rotation Hold the heel of the right foot in your left hand. Clasp the top of the foot with your right hand and rotate it in first one direction, then the other.

INDEX

Page numbers in **bold** refer to the illustrations.